# Entrepreneurs Navigating a Universe of Disruption

Gerard Anthony Reed

# Entrepreneurs Navigating a Universe of Disruption

palgrave
macmillan

Gerard Anthony Reed
Australian Film Television and Radio School (AFTRS)
Moore Park, NSW, Australia

ISBN 978-981-19-0702-9 ISBN 978-981-19-0703-6 (eBook)
https://doi.org/10.1007/978-981-19-0703-6



This Palgrave Macmillan imprint is published by the registered company Springer Nature Singapore Pte Ltd.
The registered company address is: 152 Beach Road, #21-01/04 Gateway East, Singapore 189721, Singapore

*In memory of Dr Dennis List, and my father, each of whom respectively assisted by establishing the foundations of this voyage into the unknown universe.*

# Acknowledgements

I wish to express my sincere appreciation to those who have journeyed with me over the years, and especially the recent past, and to those who will continue the journey we have begun, either with me or independently. I am also grateful to all of my students who have provided an opportunity to share this journey and to learn from their varied and diverse experiences, to an array of inspired and inspirational teachers, including my mother a schoolteacher for many decades, and to those whom I have met throughout the years, whether at school, college, institute, university, in employment or whilst travelling; to my children who always provide the greatest insight into the contemporary era, as well as a keen connectivity to the present.

With specific reference I would like to especially thank Maija Howe for ever expansive and insightful research collaborations, intriguing and productive discussions, for goal setting and reading early drafts of the work, and providing inspiring commentary, at crucial points where it has been most assisting. Jess Gillan and Andrew George for their most valuable and appreciated insights regarding the *parabolic scramble* framework usage as well as enlightening discussions across a range of relevant and applied topics. Eleanor (Elle) Cook for her loyalty and devoted friendship, Lucinda Peters for an ever-caring concern and compassion, Sophie Alstergren for her grace and humour, and my sisters, Catherine and Alice, for being always there, ever supportive and forever willing to embark upon an adventure. Peter Herbert for demonstrating expansive perspectives whilst exploring the levers of innovation, David Balfour, Jane Newton, Martin Hersov, Stephen Murphy, Dr Alejandra Canales, Melba Proestos, Maddie

Connolly, Cody Jarrett, Melanie Morningstar, Susan Danta, Dr Marty Murphy, Dr Pieter Aquilia, Dr Nell Greenwood, the generous and supportive staff of The Jerzy Toeplitz Library and my colleagues at the Australian Film Television and Radio School (AFTRS) who have assisted and facilitated the application of the *parabolic scramble* framework in a variety of ways.

To my co-researchers, Dr Liudmila (Mila) Tarabashkina, Professor Noel Lindsay, Dr Safiya Mukhtar Alshibani, Associate Professor Allan O'Connor and colleagues in research and academic pursuits, the late Dr Andrew Finegan, Dr Barry Elsey, Dr Matthew McKinlay, Professor Selva Abraham, Professor Michael Wilmore, Dr Najmeh Hassanli, Dr Graciela Corral de Zubielqui, I wish to express my gratitude for their combined knowledge, remarkable assistance with research and many important insights.

Academic editor, Barbara Brougham, has been a highly valued and consistent point of reference for me, in terms of content, and developments with an ever-evolving discussion across the submission of the manuscript for which I am also most grateful. Graphic designer, Xavier Tarren-Sweeney, for additional assistance with content formatting, layout of manuscript and responsiveness with innovative inclusions. I would also like to acknowledge Dr Vanna Morosini, who travelled the years of development and discoveries with me, including the emergent framework of the *parabolic scramble*, and was witness to much innovation and experimentation. And finally, to the future focused inspiration of the late Dr Dennis List, and the ever-innovative forward thinking of my late father, each of whom prepared the core foundations of this book, and to whom this work is dedicated.

*An artist's impression of the Voyager 2 probe entering interstellar space and a continuing journey into the unknown until it is known. (Image credit – NASA/JPL-Caltech)*

# About This Book

This book details the exploratory stages of a research study that produced a framework for entrepreneurial endeavour and enterprise. It presents an unfolding discussion, throughout its chapters, regarding the entrepreneurial nature potential within us all, and the modes by which those involved in such activity, and associated innovative discoveries, can be informed by the skills and experience already in their possession.

The book also provides, through its structure, a tool by which the entrepreneur, innovator, educator, student or those yet-to-be involved in the entrepreneurial arena can plan for the yet-to-be known eventualities of such endeavour.

The *parabolic scramble* framework is backgrounded across the discussion of entrepreneurship and the necessity to deal with the tangible and intangible of any venture, as well as other considered aspects that the entrepreneurial journey engenders.

**Image Credit: NASA**

# Contents


1 The Spirit of an Entrepreneurial Age 1

2 Establishing the Means to Navigate the Unknown 53

3 Entrepreneurs Dynamically Innovating 87

4 The Continuing Journey into the Unknown Universe 101

5 The Use of the *Parabolic Scramble* Framework 115

Appendices 125

Bibliography 131

Index 151

# About the Author

**Dr Gerard Reed** is a Senior Lecturer in Screen Business at the Australian Film Television and Radio School (AFTRS) and has experience in economic development with an emphasis on entrepreneurial and innovative screen business practices developed through post-graduate studies at The University of Adelaide's Entrepreneurship, Commercialisation and Innovation Centre (ECIC), and involvement with the South Australia Department of State Development and across industry. As subject leader, for the Master of Arts Screen: Business (MASB) and Master of Arts Screen: Business and Leadership (MASBL), Gerard actively pursues industry-related applied technological innovation inclusions for the screen and audio sector, across course materials, and their delivery.

In his professional capacity, Gerard has experience as a producer, director, writer, director of photography, editor, narrator and researcher for factual programming, with a specialisation in documentary produced formats, across platform and broadcast television applications. He has completed scripting, and production, for television documentary programming funded by the South Australian Film Corporation (SAFC), Screen Australia, Foxtel, A+E Networks International, and the Australian Broadcasting Corporation (ABC). Gerard holds a PhD in Entrepreneurship and a Master of Entrepreneurship degree from The University of Adelaide, Entrepreneurship, Commercialisation, and Innovation Centre (ECIC), a Master of Arts degree from the University of the Arts, London (UAL), and a Bachelor of Arts degree from the University of New South Wales (UNSW), Australia.

Photograph by Justine Kerrigan ACS of the author at the Australian Film Television and Radio School (AFTRS)

# Abbreviations

| | |
|---|---|
| ABC TV | Australian Broadcasting Corporation Television |
| AEE | Adelaide Entrepreneurial Ecosystem |
| AFC | Australian Film Commission |
| AFTRS | Australian Film Television and Radio School |
| AI | Artificial Intelligence |
| ANZAC | Australian and New Zealand Army Corps |
| ATO | Australian Tax Office |
| AVA | Australian Volunteers Abroad |
| BAFTA | British Academy of Film and Television Arts |
| BFI | British Film Institute |
| CMR | Computer Mediated Reality |
| ECIC | Entrepreneurship, Commercialisation and Innovation Centre |
| GMH | General Motors Holden |
| GPO | General Post Office |
| HMS | His Majesty's Ship |
| JFK | John Fitzgerald Kennedy |
| JPL | NASA Jet Propulsion Laboratory |
| LCC | London College of Communication |
| LCP | London College of Printing |
| LCPDT | London College of Printing and Distributive Trades |
| ML | Machine Learning |
| MR | Mixed Reality |
| NASA | National Aeronautics and Space Administration |
| POW | Prisoner of War |
| QAPE | Qualifying Australian Production Expense |
| REME | Royal Electrical Mechanical Engineers |
| SAFC | South Australian Film Corporation |

| | |
|---|---|
| SECRC | Senate Environment and Communications References Committee |
| SIDK | Smiths Industries Diesel Kiki Pty Ltd |
| SPA | Screen Producers Australia |
| TQM | Total Quality Management |
| UAL | University of the Arts, London |
| UNSW | University of New South Wales |
| USA | United States of America |

# List of Figures


| | | |
|---|---|---|
| Fig. 1.1 | Business Card with logo of S.I.D.K.–Smiths Industries Diesel Kiki Pty Ltd (Photograph by Author) | 7 |
| Fig. 1.2 | Envelope from S.I.D.K.–Smiths Industries Diesel Kiki Pty Ltd at Tokyo, Japan. (Photograph by Author) | 9 |
| Fig. 1.3 | *Parabolic scramble* in four dimensions as sketched. (Photograph and drawing by Author) | 10 |
| Fig. 1.4 | The Arrest of Governor William Bligh at Government House, circa 1808 | 15 |
| Fig. 1.5 | HMS Bounty mutineers turning Captain William Bligh R.N. and crew loyal to him adrift, by Robert Dodd 1790 | 16 |
| Fig. 1.6 | The NeXT Computer, Inc., on display (right of frame) at the Powerhouse Museum at Sydney, Australia. (Photograph by Author) | 18 |
| Fig. 1.7 | Systems view of creativity. (Prepared by Author based on Mihaly Csikszentmihalyi 1999) | 22 |
| Fig. 1.8 | The Kuhn Cycle (Kuhn 1970, 1996, 2011; Pajares 2013; The Kuhn Cycle 2012). (Prepared by Author) | 28 |
| Fig. 1.9 | The Kuhn Cycle (Kuhn 1970, 1996, 2011; Pajares 2013; The Kuhn Cycle 2012). (Prepared by Author) | 37 |
| Fig. 1.10 | Scramble crossing, King William Street intersecting Waymouth and Pirie Streets in the City of Adelaide. (Photograph by Author) | 42 |
| Fig. 1.11 | Notebook entries documenting the *parabolic scramble* and its potential utility. (Photograph and drawing by Author) | 44 |
| Fig. 1.12a | A police officer orchestrating the scramble crossing. (Photograph by Author) | 45 |
| Fig. 1.12b | A police officer orchestrating the scramble crossing. (Photograph by Author) | 45 |

Fig. 2.1 'Photojournal note: Sojourner spent 83 days of a planned seven-day mission exploring the Martian terrain, acquiring images, and taking chemical, atmospheric and other measurements. The final data transmission received from Pathfinder was at 10:23 UTC on September 27, 1997. Although mission managers tried to restore full communications during the following five months, the successful mission was terminated on March 10, 1998'. (Image Credit NASA/JPL) 58
Fig. 2.2 'A selfie taken by NASA's Curiosity Mars rover on Sol 2291 (January 15, 2019) at the "Rock Hall" drill site, located on Vera Rubin Ridge. This was Curiosity's 19th drill site. The drill hole is visible to the rover's lower-left; the entire scene is slightly dustier than usual due to a regional dust storm affecting the area. The selfie is composed of 57 individual images taken by the rover's Mars Hand Lens Imager (MAHLI), a camera on the end of the rover's robotic arm. The images are then stitched together into a panorama. MAHLI was built by Malin Space Science Systems, San Diego. NASA's Jet Propulsion Laboratory, a division of Caltech in Pasadena, manages the Mars Science Laboratory Project for the NASA Science Mission Directorate, Washington. JPL designed and built the project's Curiosity rover'. (Image credit: NASA/JPL-Caltech/MSSS) 59
Fig. 2.3 The action research cycle (or spiral/s) is also typical of the experience of action learning. Action learning is, however, much more associated with groups of learners or a programme of action learning within an organisation. (Prepared by Author and based on Dick 1997) 67
Fig. 2.4 Image of a scramble crossing, X-crossing or Barnes Dance. (Photograph by Author) 69
Fig. 2.5 Time-lapse delay of pedestrians using a scramble crossing (Barnes Dance). Following the time-lapse movement of the actor in the rounded yellow rectangle, we can see how a parabola can emerge as he, she, they selects an alternate route when encountering the person in orange. The actor in the blue rectangle 'dances' among the people he, she, they passes. The Barnes Dance Principle says that entrepreneurs will be faced with obstacles when attempting to reach their goals (e.g. funding), just as pedestrians face obstructions in a scramble crossing. They must react flexibly in order to avoid being blocked. They must be willing to change direction

without losing sight of their goals when faced with challenges. (Prepared by Author from a time-lapse photograph by Sam Javanrouh of a scramble crossing at Toronto, Canada sourced from:- http://wvs.topleftpixel.com/photos/2008/08/yongedundas_scramble_milestones_max_01.jpg) 70

Fig. 2.6 The *parabolic scramble* framework as part of the Barnes Dance Principle is illustrated here by the combination of circles and lines, including the wide, mauve dashed line in the shape of a parabola. The parabolic shape emerges when an individual agent decides to move differently from everyone else. Since the concept is temporal as well as physical, changes in direction or unusual movements must be compensated for in the temporal plane. (Concept and preparation by Author). 71

Fig. 3.1 Mandelbrot set as depicted by physicist Dr Wolfgang Beyer (2006) 96

Fig. 4.1 *Parabolic scramble* in four dimensions as sketched. (Photograph and drawing by Author) 102

Fig. 5.1a Alternate interpretation of movement through the *parabolic scramble*. (Image credit:- Sam Javanrouh as developed by Author) 118

Fig. 5.1b Alternate interpretation of movement through the *parabolic scramble*. (Image credit:- Sam Javanrouh as developed by Author) 118

Fig. 5.1c Alternate interpretation of movement through the *parabolic scramble*. (Image credit:- Sam Javanrouh as developed by Author) 119

Fig. 5.2 Photograph taken at Northfield Women's Prison during the *Straight-talk* documentary production. (Photograph by Author) 120

Fig. 5.3 Passport photograph of Wesley Reed during the 1970s. (Photograph by Author) 122

CHAPTER 1

# The Spirit of an Entrepreneurial Age

*Entrepreneur*, as a word or term is significant, especially if contextual to a currency of the expanding economic era where we need it to be understood, to be exclaimed, or simply and/or gently announced in a usage increasingly aligned to this epoch, or perhaps what may be described as in the spirit of an entrepreneurial age.

To detail further, though, when considering the word *entrepreneur* as a proper noun, or descriptor:

- What is its real purpose in terms of communication and outputs?
- What is it used for?
- And importantly and finally, how can we best and most effectively understand and apply it?

For those conversant with industrial revolutionary cycles, the anticipation is now, the Fourth Industrial Revolution (Schwab 2016; Schwab and Davis 2018), and much like any commonly used word, in any era, *entrepreneur* as a term grows seemingly more or less poignant with its every mention, as a paradox and its supposed familiarity, because we (collectively) become acclimated to it, and through an experience, of sorts, determine we know it. And yet, as is often the case with such usage, or supposed familiarity, we are so often left at a point, knowing less in ever decreasing cycles because the term is now a confusion of what is known, or perhaps


G. A. Reed, *Entrepreneurs Navigating a Universe of Disruption*,
https://doi.org/10.1007/978-981-19-0703-6_1

what is assumed to be known. We do know, though, that in some context, we need it to be understood effectively, towards its application.

For without a determination or universal point, as anchor or grounding, we can be cast adrift when all we really need to be aware of is how it is relevant to what we know, as individuals, contributors, activists, pacifists, antagonists, protagonists, aligning to the great expanse of whom and what we are, and what we can become. For this is perhaps the key point, as individuals to truly know our capacities in all their multi-fold and multi-role unique combinations, that make us who we are, and potential in our own right, as unique. For we are versions of many aspects of externalities (and internalities), and in turn, many of which are vast compared to our senses and sensibilities (or our capacity as humans to conceptualise this vastness).

I propose for the reader of this outline of the *entrepreneur* that there is an inherent uniqueness of the self as a combination of attributes, skills, qualities and an array of experiences that are potential, to be demonstrated from challenging, venturing forth, taking risks, learning from the spectra of epic fail, near success, total success and the myriad of experiences that you have already encountered, and make for the *entrepreneur* and your version of this term as a profound professional undertaking, or other format that is unique to you, your personality and its applications throughout a lifetime of learning. In determining and navigating the unknown, you will deal with the tangible or the intangible (to a potential range of intangibles), and the equipment you need for this is realised, to be formulated by expression or version, through your own unique understanding and format of what it is to be an *entrepreneur*.

## Scoping the Entrepreneurial Nature

We are all *entrepreneurial,* as we are, too, all inherently creative. Though this may not be considered by the individual as exemplar, as with the notion, or view towards creativity being only valid if measured against perhaps what is sometimes termed *creative genius* as the true creative application towards a perceived perfection of originality (and or, its expression). To this point it is helpful to consider the professional career of Jackson Pollack (1912–1956) with the artist's perhaps self-evident statement 'I am nature' (Levin 2013). However, at the point of this exclamation, he was defending his creative pursuit, as he embarked upon this professional undertaking as an incredibly innovative artist in modernist abstract expression that ventured into the very essence of innovative creative practice to discover the 'fingerprint of nature' in all its rawness, seemingly. However, and importantly, as evidence for Jackson Pollack's perhaps self-evident articulation of being part of an organic world, the developed and self-discovered representations of 'nature' in his work was defined post his death by Professor Benoit Mandelbrot and the latter's discovery of what would become known as the Mandelbrot set (Mandelbrot 1977, 1982; Taylor et al. 1999).

So valued are Jackson Pollack's works that they are premier in the global art market, with considerable credit being assigned to Lee Krasner (1908–1984) for her innovative marketing and ingenious understanding of the forces of supply and demand (especially across the realm of scarcity). It may seem counter-intuitive to appreciate Jackson Pollack's creative output as nature, for we are all a part of the natural world even though we may live as *homo sapiens* in urbanised or suburbanised settlements, in some cases, with little connection to the natural world, though we have formed another version of that world, to be determined how connected to nature or not, is often contentious or discursive. Jackson Pollack was a part of nature, and trusted his creative practice accordingly by his declaration of a seemingly obvious manifesto. However, there was no greater truth or seeking of the truth in that context. For any organic entity, it could be postulated or proposed for the purest form.

So, let's consider that we may be deliberate or accidental entrepreneurs, or possessing of the entrepreneurial nature or its spirit. It is just a matter of how you view this term yourself, and the potential of a contribution–profound, indeterminate or unknown until it is known.

To preface the experience of this text, it may be within your area of comfort, or perhaps outside of your experience, deliberately and importantly adventurous exploratorily, and could be questioning of your previous experience. As to the point, we are all unique as *entrepreneurs*, as entrepreneurial endeavour is indeterminate, individual, harsh, experiential, exciting, invigorating to painful potentially, and a myriad of emotional interpretations that are desirably determinate (especially contextual to those seeking certainty and the structure that may provide it), and yet, by nature indeterminate. For it is akin to any quest, the more you discover, the more you realise there is much more to discover (tempered by the fact that boundaries assist with direction of resources and energy). As with any endeavour, it is potential as an infinite exercise of exploration knowing no end (as has been realised through theoretical physics and the expanding universe). Whether it is possible to gain comfort from this notion is up to the individual, and typically is measured with the comfort one can glean from being and living with discomfort, until of course, that becomes comfortable. Perhaps we should entertain the juncture of these paradoxes as a normative state in order to be flexible and open to change.

*Becoming comfortable being uncomfortable* is the mantra I have taught repeatedly across several years of *creativity and innovation* delivered courses whether at university, business institutions or college. Design thinking and/or parallel thinking (De Bono 1992, 2016) carry notions of exploration into the unknown to then know it. These techniques provide a structure, usually in terms of a set of instructions through processes that have reflective or iterative cycles. This *mandatory discomfort* mantra I have used, and have heard used in a range of contexts, including affirmation to rules to follow when the going gets difficult. For example, the United States Navy Sea, Air and Land (SEAL) team members embrace it as part of their combined special forces tasks for Naval Special Warfare Command, which have been adapted to business applications, especially across organisational or cultural improvement (Gleeson 2018).

However, the important point that I have learnt about design thinking, and this discomfort, is that it is only part of the entrepreneur's repertoire, for there are many, and a growing multitude of experiences that the entrepreneur builds upon, to then build upon those, again, and again ad infinitum. And much like design thinking, it is but one aspect of the tools, or frameworks, that can be utilised in the course of an entrepreneurial journey. I will detail some, and introduce a framework in development that is organically designed for the entrepreneur. The *parabolic scramble* emerged from research study into entrepreneurial activity, and innovative ways to deal with paths of dependency, risk, variables and chaotic environments, amongst a range of other applications.

Design thinking, when considered as the union of business and art, provides instructional clarity regarding the nuance of intangibility in both terms. When we plan a business, or any future strategy, it is creative, even if based upon facts and evidence, especially when pre-start-up or in the conceptual phase of the business plan, whether developed for investors, or a single page outline of summary. This phase must rely upon creative projections, because in this early phase, the business most probably does not exist in a format yet. So is the case with the development of art, the work is a creative vision whether planned or expressed at the time of its creation. These are the intangibilities that now conjoin in terms of design thinking, being the union between business and art as it is utilised as a tool to discover, define, develop and then achieve delivery (Design Council 2019); and as used in terms of lean methodological rapid prototyping intended to be at little to no cost (Ries 2011) to the creator/researcher/producer and tested across human-centred design applications and principles.

## Backgrounding Innovation

Upon reflection, and only with a recent awareness as writing these pages, did I realise the extent to which I was exposed whilst a child growing up in Western Sydney, Australia, to the incremental elements of innovation, and all that is required, during development in a commercial process, and very much across the idea of production. In essence, innovation was backgrounded constantly in my formative years, although not seen as anything special. My father was consistently innovating at his workplace, as what I would later understand to be *intrapreneurial* (Frederick et al. 2019) in its nature. He completed a master's degree research project (Reed 1998) in total quality management (TQM) after a lifetime of interest in education, and became a go-to fix-it consultant in the Australian (Sydney based) automotive industry and its allied trades. He worked to streamline production processes, and compliance regulations across air conditioning development and implementation, and later brake systems for automobiles.

Throughout my childhood, I would be intrigued by the array of prototypes my father would bring home to show my family what he had produced with engineers, and always in the capacity of manufacturing. In Australia, this was a time of contracting protection for secondary industry that was buffeted by economic rationalisation, and a realisation of competitive global markets, across the waves and ripples of economic recession and its recovery. The prototypes to note were not necessarily related to the automotive industry per se, as what I realise now was that my father's firm was experimenting across a broad range of market offerings, including electric motor assembly kits, heating units, rubberised plastics for use in a variety of consumables, to concepts replacing wooden pallets in factories with alternatives. Everything was open to be improved, and as my father specialised in TQM, this became even more pronounced and innovative, as he used the discipline of this framework to review and seek improvements through all stages of the production process, at all times.

Many years later, as adjunct to doctoral research studies, I would investigate elements of the motor vehicle industry in South Australia, as General

Motors Holden (GMH) moved towards a withering conclusion. The research study was for the South Australia Department of State Development led by Dr Allan O'Connor at The University of Adelaide, Entrepreneurship, Commercialisation, and Innovation Centre (ECIC), which heralded an ending era as GMH finally closed its doors permanently at the Elizabeth plant. My father had been to meetings at GMH and associated automotive concerns in the time I lived at Adelaide, South Australia, and he would arrive a day or so early and prepare extensively for the meetings. He often asked to drive to the location the day before, to be certain of its geography, and to diminish the possibility of being delayed in any manner, through his characteristically meticulously preparation.

It could be said that my father was a business enthusiast. However, I believe he was an innovator in his own right, and often a contrarian, as he liked the plight of the underdog, or David and Goliath (Samuel 17:1–25:7) scenarios as they offered the challenge of greatness by overcoming the formidable or seemingly overwhelming odds, I believe. Wesley was definitely an optimist who experienced the kindness and harshness of corporate enterprise, which offered a liberation of varying sorts, providing greater opportunities as his organisational skills and innovative abilities were assets that were traded with lucrative offers, both in terms of remunerations in kind and quality of experiential growth.

The 1980s would be for my childhood a consistent exposure to innovative practices in manufacturing contexts, with my father through his experience and professional expertise able to re-configure bespoke production processes in their entirety to be more efficient. Wesley would work for a subsidiary of a joint venture by an English and Japanese company, Smiths Industries Diesel Kiki Pty Ltd, respectively, the subsidiary just being known by its acronym in our family and said often, SIDK. The logo he designed, as he'd also once been a draughtsman, in the spirit of the joint venture and as depicted in Fig. 1.1, was also a feature of my childhood as my father drove us to the SIDK premises in Guildford, Sydney, to view the newly erected signage depicting his created logo for the joint venture. For Wesley, his work was all-consuming; it seemed to a child growing up in the industrial corporate landscape, observing a life that seemed to be dedicated to a world foreign to children who would only ever know it as an observer of signage and innovative prototypes. Never venturing with his children beyond the perimeter of the industrial complex, the genesis of these innovative creations remained a secret to the observing children.

**Fig. 1.1** Business Card with logo of S.I.D.K.–Smiths Industries Diesel Kiki Pty Ltd (Photograph by Author)

My father's formative years in Australia, though, as a recent immigrant from Britain, would see a variety of occupations aligned to an engineering basis, including Australian Electrical Industries Pty. Limited., which built upon a background in the former country, including the General Electric Company and Osram Lamp Works. He trained as a fitter and turner, having completed an apprenticeship with Bren Manufacturing Co. Ltd. (began at 16 years of age and would include 2 years at Durham Chemicals Limited.), before serving in Cyprus as a member of the British Army's Royal Electrical Mechanical Engineers (REME) Light Aid Detachment (LAD) during the period of the Suez Crisis in 1956.

Wesley's father, my grandfather, had been a Prisoner of War (POW) at Wolfsberg (Stalag XVIIIA) in Austria, having been wounded at The Second Battle of El Alamein in 1942, and survived to be captured at The Battle of Primosole Bridge in Sicily on 17 July 1943 by paratroopers or Fallschirmjager (known as 'Green Devils' colloquially) of the Luftwaffe.

After an end of war dash for the Allied lines with two other POWs, one of whom was presumed killed in an encounter with Wehrmacht elements, my grandfather, Ernest, joined the Royal Engineers and became a sapper. This being strategically pursued by Ernest in order to gain the necessary skills needed for post-war civilian resettlement in an anticipated competitive labour market. He was repatriated into industry in the North-East of England. Formerly, he had been a labourer with the prospect of being employed either digging clay to make bricks or working on a farm, with a fall-back position of the mines.

The notion of business, engineering and Australia were almost entwined for my father as I join his dots. Ernest became good mates with imprisoned Australian service personnel at Wolfsberg Stalag XVIIIA, one in particular, a former solicitor, now an imprisoned sergeant, who said often 'Ernie, you have to come out to Oz'.

Wesley would become an enthusiastic and dedicated immigrant to Australia and an optimist no matter the variance of experiences this new life would bring, forever open to expansive possibilities (Fig. 1.2). For the purposes of this narrative, and what strikes me after so many years, especially subsequent to my father's death more than a decade past, is that he was involved in a form of lean manufacturing (Blank 2013; Cooper and Vlaskovits 2016; Ries 2011). This developed as a format for contemporary *entrepreneurs* involved in rapid prototyping across human-centred design applications. Lean manufacturing as developed in Japan, especially the Toyota Production System (Toyota 2020), was concerned with the refinement of process and importantly became a philosophical position for management. Efforts centred on the elimination of waste from the production endeavour. This manufacturing process being developed and perfected at the withering conclusion of the Third Industrial Revolutionary cycle though at heightened and perfected levels of efficiencies.

The format of this book will follow that of a new framework which is designed to be central to it, the *parabolic scramble*, and importantly provide its theoretical and philosophical structure which, if appreciated in part at the commencement of this text, will assist with its progressive revelation. This was sketched and developed in a variety of iterations across many notebooks, as displayed in Fig. 1.3.

I have increasingly become aware of innovative thinkers as the years have passed, my father Wesley included, especially across history when considering a range of alternative thinkers through their creative practice. Whether artists, writers, engineers, politicians, health practitioners,

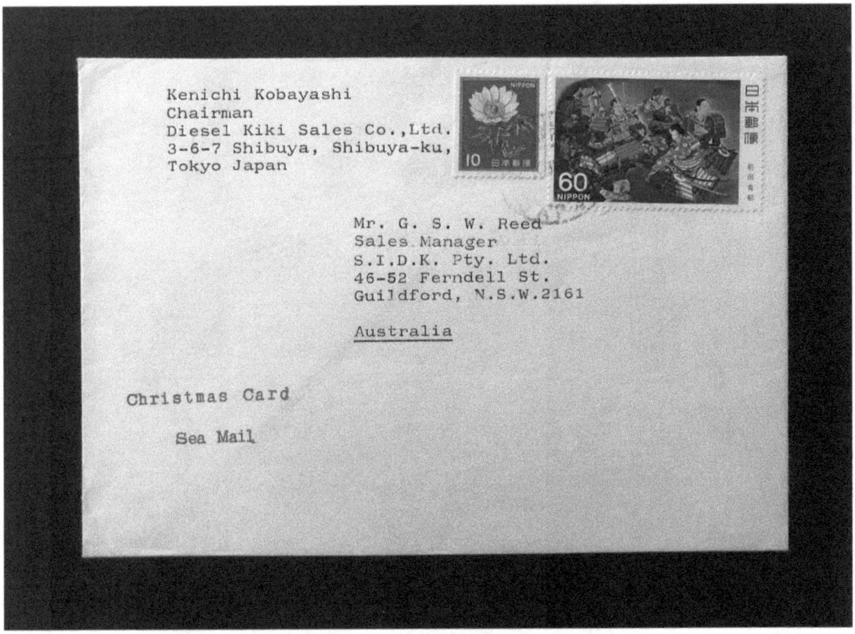


**Fig. 1.2** Envelope from S.I.D.K.–Smiths Industries Diesel Kiki Pty Ltd at Tokyo, Japan. (Photograph by Author)

business people or workers/creators in any capacity, there is an inherent creativity that is notable. In even the most seemingly menial of tasks, there is to be found creativity.

Whilst working a variety of jobs to support my postgraduate studies in London, England, a colleague, many years my senior, described the ability of one of her siblings to wash clothes by hand like no other person that she knew. The sibling, as described, was artful and creative in the washing of clothing and this struck my imagination at the time and since. It was described vividly and was illustrative of a previous era, and lives on to be recorded here because of that outstanding and creative talent (that perhaps otherwise may go unrecorded and or/unnoticed except by those in immediate comparison of her remarkable talent and skill when embarking upon such essential endeavour) now replaced, in the most part, by machines.

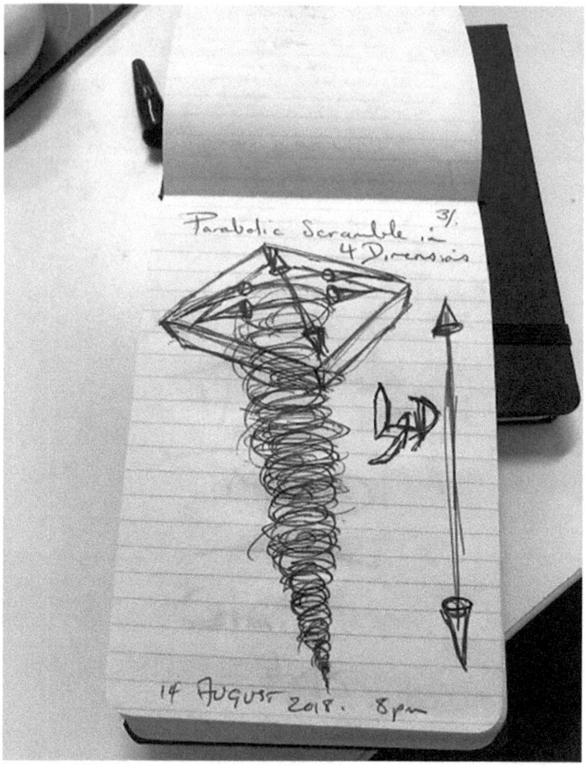


**Fig. 1.3** *Parabolic scramble* in four dimensions as sketched. (Photograph and drawing by Author)

Though we may use machines to enhance our lives, increasingly there is to be remembered the labour that they save us from, and for which we would find our skill and aptitude increasingly based upon an inherent ability to understand and be creative in such pursuits. And to this application I have been drawn to attempt to appreciate, for it is probably impossible to really understand, the creative process towards creative practice of an organic and living entity. We are surrounded by creativity in all its myriad and varied forms, but because it becomes every day, we are not transfixed by its uniqueness and inherent characteristics that should otherwise inspire awe.

## Backgrounding Empathy and Creativity

When I discovered a wallet belonging to a former soldier of the German Imperial Army of World War One (WWI), I had no notion that this was to be my introduction to wartime souveniring, and therefore the works of Professor Bill Gammage (1974). I would correspond with and later interview this wonderfully inspired, insightful and courageous historian. I also drew inspired insights from Professor Eugene B. Sledge (1981), formerly of the United States Navy 1st Marine Division, veteran of Peleliu and Okinawa, whose memoir *With the Old Breed* detailed souveniring, as had Bill Gammage's *The Broken Years: Australian Soldiers in the Great War* (1974). These direct and visceral texts, respectively, provided illumination as I attempted to gain clarity across a relatively sensitive (as it would transpire as I attempted to seek institutional understanding of souveniring on this somewhat under-discussed or represented area of service personnel in areas of conflict) topic of endeavour during war.

Ken Burns and Lynn Novack's documentary series *The War,* (2007) and *The Vietnam War* (2017) details war souveniring in the Pacific Theatre of Operations and the lack of empathy for an enemy in the latter also, in a manner not dissimilar. Regarding the formidable civil war that took place in Vietnam (Burchett 1977) with international elements, it is notable that the conflict in Indochina spilled over into North American society, and seemed to almost rip the fabric of that society apart.

It is of interest and notable that empathy, as such a key factor in design thinking and human-centred design, and the lack of it, is also key to the conflict of human societies, for it is in the empathic arena that connection is formed. When connection, through a lack of empathy, is not present, then it is possible to detach from, if not de-construct, the opposing human and their humanity, be it personal or party, and/or their respective interest. All organic forms have needs in order to exist, and when co-existent in social-political systems of continuity, human beings have distinct requirements, which may in some cases seem oppositional, and yet, when empathy is brought in, then need or needs become apparent, and a connection is formed. In the case of war, as depicted by Eugene Sledge (1981), the point the author makes in terms of the taking of souvenirs, especially regarding the taking of gold amalgam teeth fillings from the corpses or the dead and in a documented case, the still living, is stark in its linkages to the abandonment of civilisation. The road back from where civilisation was abandoned on those islands and atolls of the *South West Pacific Area (command)*, by Eugene Sledge, would be long and arduous to result in a remarkable memoir that was assistant to his psychological recovery of trauma derived from war, towards the recovery of what can be considered to be moral injury (Meagher 2014).

In *The Fog Of War: Eleven Lessons From The Life of Robert S. McNamara* (2003), the first lesson detailed by the former Secretary of State of the United States of America (USA) relates directly to the Cuban Missile Crisis of 16–28 October 1962, during which the Cold War moved dramatically to a Hot War designation, potentially a third world war, which was remarkably abated. The first lesson was to *empathise with your enemy*, which Robert Strange McNamara (1916–2009) details in terms of the Vietnamese people. However, in this first of the 11 lessons, initially the context of the Cuban Missile Crisis is used to demonstrate where the empathy of a former USA Ambassador to Moscow, Llewellyn E. (Tommy) Thompson (1904–1972), persuaded President John Fitzgerald Kennedy (JFK) (1917–1963) and the governing administration to consider the softer of two messages received from the Union of Soviet Socialist Republics (USSR), on behalf of Nikita Khrushchev (1894–1971), regarding a way to avert the potential offensive confrontation posed by the Soviet missiles in Cuba. So, interestingly and importantly, the world was saved, according to Robert McNamara by an empathetic understanding of the so-called enemy.

As is revealed in the documentary by Robert McNamara, former USA Ambassador, Llewellyn Thompson and his spouse Jane Monroe Thompson (née Goelet) (1921–1999) had visited the Khrushchev household (Thompson and Thompson 2018) where they had been guests, and therefore understood the leader of the USSR as a person and with empathy. With such a personal understanding of the leader, during a Cold War where a state of suspended hostility stood ready, the end of civilisation as we know it was not ushered in. The point is made by Robert McNamara that this was not to be the case with the Vietnam War (1955–1975), where an appreciation of the enemy could have potentially altered the course of its history.

In the broader scope of gaining an understanding of hominids, as we moved over tens of thousands of solar returns on Earth, to develop the mores of human-centred groupings, with the rules that then developed as normative ethical behaviours, the seeking of harmony or perfection in these human systems whereby the basis is the safety and security of its members in terms of physical, spiritual and emotional continuity. To this objective, it can be seen there have been many attempts in human-centric societies to institute a holistic system of order that is deemed at the time of its creation to be correct and right. The notion though that we can have a perfection of sorts is perhaps the point (and its potential flaw if the notion remains static), for it is the constant revision of the system that is requisite as history has demonstrated.

Whether a manifesto, of which there have been consistently magnificent attempts to equate the rights of humans with an all-encompassing and inclusive order of care towards liberty of body and soul (of self-identified species, and other sentient beings) (WWF Global 2013), there perhaps cannot be the panacea without a constant and consistent iterative revision. This is really the essence of a renewal that is necessary in all aspects of human society and endeavour, with an acknowledgement that perfection may not be achievable or even possible. For it is not that we seek the perfect incorruptible state, for as organic beings, decay is a part of the order of continuation. Premature decay is not necessary, and if preventable and conscious can be anticipated and recovered from, in essence, a healing of the organic entity.

To the greater realisation and its point, after examining the many manifestos of human society, whether political, social or other, I resolved that no one manifesto or belief was, or could be, representative. However, when taken as a group, there were elements that could be beneficial at differing times, and at different locations, from the myriad of diverse and eclectic sources. There was almost a reconstitution that was essential to understand the requirements of time (Blank 2018) and this moment, to then customise accordingly. The *parabolic scramble* is an attempt to draw the many inputs together, with the notion that perfection or the ultimate solution is not possible, for it is in the striving of the most appropriate application at this moment that is the point, and we draw from a diverse and divergent palette, to a convergence of those elements.

When considering what it is to be an *entrepreneur,* there is a range of terms historically, internationally and cross-culturally (Frederick et al. 2019) that can be used to define this process, application, as personal attributes, or seemingly defined characteristics. However, as with most individuals, it is the first instance of exposure that is usually the most lasting and influential, and, in terms of contemplating the accidental entrepreneur, and what this entails, I explain my own context to provide some illumination on the genesis of a journey that continues; and is relevant to the undertaking of this book as a text to accompany those entertaining, embarking upon or involved with entrepreneurial endeavour.

## The Accidental Entrepreneur?

The very first exposure to the word *entrepreneur* begins with a transportation in terms of European settlement, and in particular British settlement, amidst the nervous rivalry of nations during an imperial age with territorial acquisition, on the continent of Australia. Convicts to the new penal colony during the late eighteenth and early to mid-nineteenth centuries, to be established at Botany Bay were indeed transported. My own transportation to a school history lesson, in my early teens, was my first encounter with the French-derived word *entreprendre* (to undertake, amidst other variations, such as initiate, begin, start, make and a myriad of others potentially), which was used to describe the character of an earlier New South Wales Corp officer [formerly 68th (Durham) Regiment of Foot (Light Infantry)] Lieutenant John Macarthur (1767–1834), in part, and a reputation linked to a seemingly, as represented in the context of the lesson, self-interested colonial commercial exploitation. This was later further linked to the dramatic removal, through Australia's only recorded 'successful' military coup, (during which time Macarthur was no longer operating as a military official) of the serving colonial governor, Captain William Bligh R.N. (Royal Navy) (1754–1817).

By the stage that William Bligh was being famously documented in caricature attempting to seemingly evade those deposing him during the Rum Rebellion (Evatt 1955) by hiding under his bed at Government House (41 Bridge Street, Sydney), as depicted in Fig. 1.4, which is questionably ill-founded on fact, he had already lost His Majesty's Ship (HMS) or His Majesty's Armed Vessel Bounty to a mutiny some distance off the shores of Tahiti in the South Pacific, with the deposing in that instant being far more serious in the context of the risk to his life, and that of his supporters, depicted in Fig. 1.5. They were collectively cast adrift (as depicted by artist Robert Dodd shortly afterwards in the 1790 painting) in a crowded open boat, with the unstated intention that they should perish.

One member did die quite soon afterwards in an incident at Tofua. However, Lieutenant William Bligh famously navigated and mapped the Endeavour Strait, and part of the north-east coast of New Holland, as it was then known, completing a journey of 3 618 nautical miles or 6 700 kilometres to reach Timor (Alexander 2003). Notably for the process of

**Fig. 1.4** The Arrest of Governor William Bligh at Government House, circa 1808

entrepreneurial endeavour, Bligh was wanting to be successful as a famous explorer, as he had served with Captain James Cook (1728–1779) (Hough 1994). But he would feel the weight of a defeat, that in the historical context of survival and leadership is now deemed to be exemplary. William Bligh's life is exemplary for a range of reasons often linked to the two mutinies and yet, when gauging the personal characteristics of the individual, in adversity it can be said that he was a remarkably brave, and a resolute leader of profound qualities and distinct integrity and determination in the face of *extremis.* This was like Ernest Shackleton (1874–1922), who similarly completed an equally remarkable open boat journey of 720 nautical miles, or 1333 kilometres (in the extreme conditions of an Antarctic winter).

When considering innovation, I often think of the examples of William Bligh and Ernest Shackleton, historical figures now who were very much focused upon ambitious outcomes that would not be achievable due to the profound nature of circumstances at the juncture of their opportunity and endeavours. These immense eventualities would frustrate the ambition of both William Bligh and Ernest Shackleton by providing the most profound of obstacles, really in terms of their own survival, and the

**Fig. 1.5** HMS Bounty mutineers turning Captain William Bligh R.N. and crew loyal to him adrift, by Robert Dodd 1790

survival of those whom they led, and yet they did lead with such exemplary stoicism in the face of adversity and imminence of death in the obscurity of a vast oceanic expanse. William Bligh would demonstrate this indirectly in his famous *Notebook* (Bligh, Bach and National Library of Australia 1987), being concerned that his demise would result in the loss of a pension for his wife and family due to the loss of the HMS Bounty, a potential court-martial offence under military law.

As I would learn, in due course, of the leadership qualities of William Bligh and Ernest Shackleton, so too would that distant history lesson be my guide to the *entrepreneur* until I learnt that, like John Macarthur, William Bligh and Ernest Shackleton, we can all be innovators, exemplary in our pursuits, especially when tested by adversity, albeit in a much different context, and era, and potentially in differing ways. For everyone awakening to this fact, although it may seemingly be by accident, the truth is always there, waiting to be discovered by the individual, whether a long-ago history lesson, or otherwise, as when the presentation is correct for the student to absorb. That is the moment of learning.

As co-founder of Apple Inc., Steve Jobs (1955–2011) famously detailed in his Stanford Graduation Keynote Address (2005) that it is possible to join the dots when looking into the past, but not the case when reviewing, or tracking, into the future. And to this point I reflect upon the diverse and eclectic education I received during my school years, in particular from a self-identifying cohort of teachers at my junior secondary school, Oakhill College, located near the north-western Sydney suburb of Castle Hill, whom had collectively been involved as Australian Volunteers Abroad (AVA) in a scheme that enabled them to be placed overseas on specialised programmes.

The teachers would describe their experiences overseas, and importantly it informed a lot of additional material that we would be taught that was specific to the culture of peoples in other countries to which the respective teachers had been exposed, and then, importantly, the culture of peoples in Australia. We were taught about the historical impact of British and European settlement on the continent of Australia (when ranging across the vast acreage of the school grounds during class-bound excursions on-site) and the displacement of the original inhabitants. Additional consideration was given with regard to the removal of these peoples from their respective lands, such as detailed in the history of Tasmania. Their society was completely dismantled and relocated in remnants to ultimately be devastatingly and tragically almost extinguished as the cultural continuum of a people, who had been inhabiting that land mass, formerly a promontory of the continent. These educational dots were to be foundational to future endeavour, including remarkable exposure to photography, art, music and drama provided by a group of dedicated and inspiring teachers.

To return to Steve Jobs and his Stanford Graduation Keynote Address (2005) and the importance of joining the dots, he would also detail the struggles, trials and tribulations that would be the making of Apple Inc. The future revitalisation of the company that he was forced to leave and come back to would need the NeXT Computer, Inc., to be developed as seen in Fig. 1.6, before revitalisation was to be possible.

The NeXT Inc. computer workstation would not make the sales Steve Jobs had anticipated, nor be the great alternative to Apple Inc. products that he had designed it to be. It would instead be the engine of the second wave of Apple Inc. products as no other had been. The NeXT Inc. computer, or operating system, would also enable the World Wide Web (WWW)

**Fig. 1.6** The NeXT Computer, Inc., on display (right of frame) at the Powerhouse Museum at Sydney, Australia. (Photograph by Author)

or Internet to be possible earlier than otherwise, so had a profound global effect.

So, what are the dots that I can consider to detail the journey to this moment that may provide some insight as to the motivations behind these writings? As it turns out, there are many potential aspects, qualities and attributes that align with what it is to be an *entrepreneur*. And, like John Macarthur, not all of it is predictable, for I'm sure if you told him that he would one day be involved in a military coup at Port Jackson, later known in the greater geographical context as Sydney, he would have wondered about the implications of such a future.

The journey for any entrepreneur, or adventurer, can involve risk, and it is the risk that provides the opportunity. However, if not guarded or ameliorated against, risk can be the destruction of the project, enterprise or potentially the person, and can be described to be *persistent destruction*. It was explained anecdotally to me by a key facilitator (Daly 2013) in an

Adelaide Entrepreneurial Ecosystem (AEE) study I was co-researching with Dr Allan O'Connor (now Associate Professor), of an informal meeting of entrepreneurs in the city of Adelaide, who, now successful, spoke about 'failure' as a theme of their meeting. It was apparently a deeply moving and emotional experience for all involved as they relived their struggles against adversity, with a variety of less than successful outcomes at the time, for which they could now contextualise and accept, though the painful residue of those experiences remained in varying degrees.

The journey that I embarked upon from an early age was one of optimism and exploration at all stages that I recall, everything a possibility or an opportunity of fantastic adventure from my earliest memories. Escaping over the gas metre box to run down the street, or unlocking the side gate latch with a broom, always trying to get out of the containment of my existence to see what was possible elsewhere. My band of neighbourhood friends, who would be allies in the many projects I carved out of my early years, ranged over the seemingly ever-expansive acreage of suburbia and bushland in my picturesque and historic hilly environment of North Rocks in Sydney, Australia.

There was a majestic element to these early years encapsulated in a playful exploration that would live with me into adulthood, to become a part of any endeavour, whether menial or otherwise. I would travel a world at peace, and briefly at war, as a young man, without much expectation, and yet the instilled belief that anything was possible, and really it was in so many different ways. Without any conception of my destiny, I worked on beaches in Greece in my Australian-made King Gee shirt and shorts, with Blundstone steel cap boots that came in handy when walking up and down the flat stone covered beaches, some as small as saucers, and others as big as plates. These were fine for the Island of Samos, however problematic when crossing from the Sinai Peninsula across Taba into Eilat and the bristling sensitivity of the metal detectors. Security staff had to endure handling boots that had been on my feet for weeks at a time, with little opportunity to bath in the desert, or on the roads which I travelled usually on my own. I remember meeting many influential individuals on my travels and one, an English mother of grownup children, whom I befriended with her husband whilst collecting deck chair fare on a beach in Greece, memorable for the statement, '... you must have been brought up well to have such confidence to travel as you do ...'. I had not thought about it as such. I just assumed everyone was like me, and could do what I did, and, of course, they could have. I would realise as the years passed, that it was a freedom of mind and spirit that I cherished, almost as much as my innate sense of adventure and playful exploration. Everything was of interest potentially and all was therefore possible.

I would occupy a couple of caves on the Island of Samos at the eastern Aegean Sea, with a view of Turkey across the narrow Mycale Strait. Later I was isolated in the deserts of the Middle East, at distinct border country, and found a profound freedom of self and an exploration of creativity and spirit that was indicative of the environment and fuelled by it. The sense of awe was carried as a great gift that inspired a life to be lived and was really a positivity of the present, future and the past. A living past informed as was relevant, or important, and potentially influential in the positive or negative. There were indeed some things that could be problematic as I became more discerning, and yet, I was never crossed with tragedy as others I would meet and know were. I was in a way fortuitous not to possess a negative appraisal of situations and circumstances, for negativity would take the lives of some of those closest to me, and blight others whom I'd known with the ever-present past pain or injury as an eternal burden.

I was proud of my steadfastness when duty called and felt honoured to stand shoulder to shoulder with those who battled demons past and present. However, I would learn through this experience that their perspective was separate, and as real as it could be to them, and although I would empathise with them, it was not possible to be my perception at any stage. It was a great lesson regarding the independence, and clarity of self, required to be a good witness. My attitude to life remained unaltered in its optimism and exploration of the possibility of all, and this is how I now look at the future, and view the present, and of course, the past also as and where relevant.

## The Entrepreneurial Spirit Is Potential in Us All

For several years now, I have taught the subject 'Creativity and Innovation' in a range of business contexts and at a variety of universities and institutions. I have taught up to 40 plus students at a time and had many occasions where people from a diverse range of backgrounds have approached me individually to explain that they were not in any way 'creative'. They universally have bravely trusted me with this disclosure, and whenever I've encountered this revelation I know they have the potential to be the most successful in the courses I have run. We are all inherently creative, and the point of the offering is to activate, actually reactivate, this essential component as requisite for the 'innovation' that I believe we are all capable of.

The renowned author of entrepreneurial insight and transformation Professor Saras Sarasvathy, along with co-author Professor Sankaran Venkataraman (2011), wrote a remarkably transformative paper concerning the use of entrepreneurship as a method, by positioning it as akin to the scientific method in the natural realm as formulated, in its formative era, by Francis Bacon (1561–1626). The scientific method, the authors put forward, was instrumental to the success of the Industrial Revolution. In a similar way they posit open questions to assist with the development of future revolutionary possibilities in terms of technological, societal, commercial and other undertakings. In my considerations of the screen sector, I have consistently been reviewing applications of technology, narrative and story across existent and emergent applications relevant to the visual and sonic realm. So, too, do the domains of practice in creativity feature, as they must increasingly, as the entrepreneur, protagonist, antagonist, artist, craftsperson, professional operates in their respective domains.

The nature of psychologist Mihaly Csikszentmihalyi's (1999) systems view of creativity as detailed in Fig. 1.7 can be utilised to appreciate another aspect of entrepreneurship in terms of creative practice across many disciplines and fields of study whether operational, commercial or otherwise. Notably, Mihaly Csikszentmihalyi, with Barbara Frederickson and Christopher Peterson as co-developers and researchers in this field of psychology, initiated in the late 1990s, sought to present psychology as something other than defined by the treatment of malady, trauma or other illness states. Their concept became known as positive psychology.

Csikszentmihalyi (2004) determines and details through his research the constituent elements of the creative practitioner and their creative practice, which was initially focused upon artists and scientists whose objective was not fame or fortune but rather creative output. This may be extended to the astrophysicist, industrial designer, automobile maker or any range of economic or creative pursuit. This can be brought into the creative practice of an individual, team, or organisation, institution or other, in terms of iterative processes.

Importantly, for anyone involved in the creative *Field* in conjunction with *Domain* and *Individual* as depicted in Fig. 1.7, whether perceiving themselves as an entrepreneur or not, there is an iterative process that takes place as we build upon the past experiments and adventures in form and practice. In many ways this iterative process is akin to the scientific

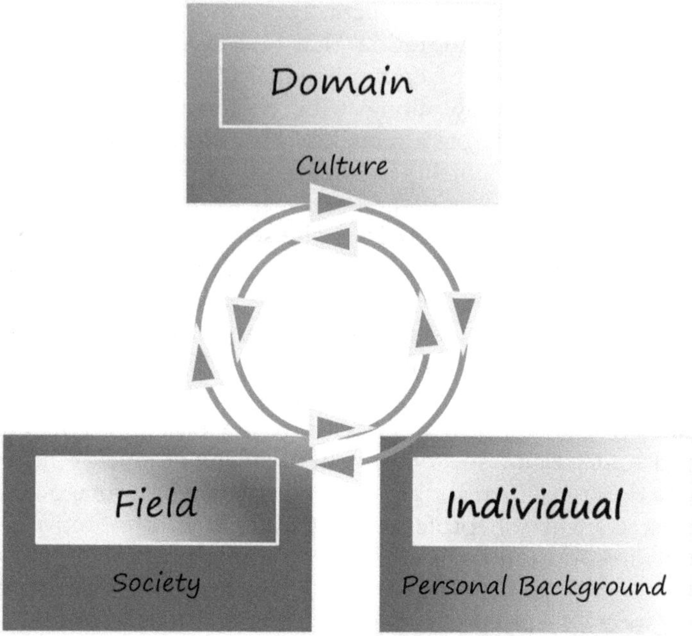


**Fig. 1.7** Systems view of creativity. (Prepared by Author based on Mihaly Csikszentmihalyi 1999)

method of hypothesis testing, whereby the results may be eternally inconclusive. Consider the prospect of placing the distinct constituents of the Milky Way Galaxy in a laboratory to test them, and yet theoretical astrophysicists creatively derive research outputs consistently with profound and resolute impacts across human societal constructs. Considering the trust involved in being confident with creative practice is understanding the self, and sense of self, being comfortable with it and owning it with agency, an agency that is practised, and reformatted, trusted, and then practised again, and again. These are the iterations of creative practice.

Emotional intelligence plays its part here, and the building of a resilience that provides a protective balance to the creative process. This lends itself to the creative practice and essentially feeds back into it, as part of a building or constructive capital in a sense. In terms of creative practice and its iterations, these rotations or cycles of endeavour build upon what is presented at any given time, considering that there may be an abundance of resources, or perhaps a little too few, many potential team members or collaborators, or none. It is in the *Flow* that Csikszentmihalyi details (1999, 2004), that flow is part of this conceptually, in terms of the iterations needed to break into a domain or field, it is completed iteratively, depending upon the resistance of the gatekeepers, or alternatively, the lack of resistance.

## Innovation, Is it Creativity or Opportunity That Fuels it?

When considering creativity, it can be helpful to position it in terms of opportunity, either the opportunity we give ourselves or others. Entrepreneurship, when placed in this context, enables the actor, or agent, to initiate the creation of opportunity on many levels, the opportunity that we give ourselves and others, the opportunity to meet a need or want in economic society, or as social capital or other.

In terms of creativity and opportunity (as the fuel of innovation), I would often think about it in terms of the work I completed across the criminal justice system in South Australia after returning from travels overseas, and settling in Adelaide.

I specialised in Documentary whilst completing a Master of Arts degree in Independent Film and Video, practically and theoretically, at the London College of Printing and Distributive Trades (LCPDT) as part of the London College of Printing (LCP) or London College of Communications (LCC), and the greater umbrella organisation of the London Institute, now an amalgamation of all the Art Colleges in London, being currently constituent as the University of Arts, London (UAL). This course of study followed an undergraduate degree at the University of New South Wales (UNSW), where I was part of a student elected team which ran a television station UNI-TV and broadcast to a footprint of 30, 000, including the student population of the UNSW, and out to the suburb of Randwick in Sydney and nearby beach areas. I spent about 60 hours a week making student-related programming covering protests, student affairs, extending to issue-based magazine studio programmes, such as the Arab Israeli Dispute, Environmental Issues, Religion and a range of documentaries and original and adapted (The Brothers Grimm tale of the *Devil with the Three Golden Hairs*) drama projects.

I had not intended doing any further study after graduating from UNSW, nor had I focused upon a future of travel, which I did as an accidental traveller. I would travel throughout Europe and work where I could find it, eventually ending up in the Arava (or Arabah) desert on the Border with Jordan (as part of the Jordan Rift Valley) as forces massed in the Middle East in preparation for a war against the Iraqi regime, following the invasion of Kuwait in 1990. It was in northern Israel when on a day's leave from a Moshav, that I passed a tree on an open plain, with parachutists descending at a nearby airfield. As I rode past on a bicycle, I instinctively had to stop and go back to the tree. I walked up to it and held its leaves in my hands and smelled the wonderful aroma of eucalyptus which was like an elixir from home (and the commencement of a profound type of homesickness).

This was the beginning of a return to Australia that took years. I realised I was committed to Australia, despite a British heritage, when living with a Londoner in the Arava or Arabah (وادي عربة, *Wādī 'Araba, Wadi Arava or Jordan Rift Valley*) desert. He had been brought up on Hampstead Heath, with a hint of Rastafarianism, complete with well cared for dreadlocks, echoing his Jamaican heritage. I realised that he was far more English than I could ever be, and I was as English, as much as he was Jamaican. We were the children of migrants. That was our commonality mostly and our differences were cultural. He was culturally English and I was culturally Australian. Our historical reference points were once removed, and the culturally embedded qualities of our societies were what we now carried into a profound isolation in the desert compound of the Moshav that we now occupied, as war stirred, and ultimately was unleashed across the area.

I returned to Britain and undertook screen studies at Birkbeck College, University of London, later being accepted onto a Master of Arts degree programme in Independent Film and Video, after I completed a short film in London with friends from Northern Ireland called *Eddie Get It!* (1991). I then began writing film reviews and completed interviews with independent film-makers and film-making institutions, such as Four Corners in Bethnal Green. I would cut film there and conduct research at the British Film Institute (BFI) concerning the origins of filmic documentary watching early Robert Flaherty (1884–1951) and John Grierson's (1898–1972) General Post Office (GPO) Unit films on a *Steenbeck* flatbed lacing 35 mm prints across its sprockets and viewing system. I attended the British Academy of Film and Television Arts (BAFTA) at Piccadilly Circus and would watch newly released features there on numerous occasions, as well as attend bespoke pre-viewing cinemas provided by distributors, as I prepared reviews for publication of commercial and independent cinema offerings prior to their release to the public.

So, I would eventually return to Australia and enjoy living in Adelaide, had a remarkable mezzanine loft, which had recently been a produce storage warehouse, as a studio with my partner Vanna Morosini at Rundle Street's East End Market. While there, I made a series of short films, including *East Market Ends* in 1994, wrote a variety of drafts of varying length, short-, medium- and long-form scripts, and continued to complete cinema reviews and articles for street media, until I eventually started to get established in the screen sector, and began making documentaries in the criminal justice system.

Many of the prisoners, or detainees, we worked with became excellent crew members, after we completed therapy with them in sessions conducted by a wonderfully enlightened and compassionate prison manager, who was also a psychologist. It was a privilege to have this experience and meet such an array of people, with whom we shared a bond of reflection and open honesty through the group therapy sessions conducted at the prison over a series of weeks. We could have a meeting with the South Australia Minister for Correctional Services in the morning and be with serving detainees videoing projects in the afternoon, as crew or subjects, and often worked late into the evening.

## *Missing: Presumed Dead*, a Journey from the Past to Present to the Past Again

The story of *Missing: Presumed Dead* starts in the past, and moves to the future, and then moves back to the past again. It begins with a missing part of history, the loss of a man at war, a man who had a context which was rich in its place and love of him. This man's loss echoed down through the years, which became decades, then more than a century. The loss is in some way resolved as our family now knows what happened to him after I embarked upon a research journey across many agencies, local, national and international. I found an actual contemporary witness account of what had taken place in the aerial conflict over France between my relative, Pat Murphy's, aircraft and those of the Flying Circus. The Flying Circus was Rittmeister Manfred Albrecht Freiherr von Richthofen's (1892–1918) fighter wing unit (Jagdgeschwader 1), famous for their colourful aircraft designs. Though Rittmeister von Richthofen had been killed just under a month earlier than this event, dying on 21 April 1918 not far from where the account below took place on 15 May 1918.

> *The leader … was flying a triplane with a scarlet body and black wings. White-edged Maltese crosses showed up vividly on the latter. The machines either side of him were triplanes too. The one on the left had a pale-green body with yellow wings, the other was striped black-and-white. … Then a red light went up from [Napier and Murphy's Bristol fighter] … diving on the leader … the air was filled with the roaring of the engines and the rattling of the guns … then a Bristol spun slowly past me. Black smoke was streaming from it and almost immediately burst into flame. This must have been [Napier and Murphy's Bristol fighter] … I shot a glance over the side … caught a glimpse of a blazing ball of fire which … was [Napier and Murphy's] Bristol. (Voss* 1977, *204–205)*

The evolving documentary *Missing: Presumed Dead* begins with the discovery of a wallet in a collector's shop in the city of Adelaide that I made by chance as I was going to have my shoes mended. The wallet had belonged to a German soldier from WWI, being evident by his military uniform. Touchingly, the personal nature of the wallet with its numerous written enclosures made me contemplate the importance and responsibility of returning such documents to their context, whereby much like the detail recorded above, provides a resolution to the inconclusive nature of the missing determination, as a status of being.

In hindsight, and when connecting the dots, *Missing: Presumed Dead* was transformational as an entrepreneurial venture. It later became a South Australia Film Corporation (SAFC) and Australian Broadcasting Corporation (ABC) financed script prior to Screen Australia and additional ABC financing, before screening on ABC TV Channels 1 & 2, and Foxtel's History as a special featured documentary for Australian New Zealand Army Corps (ANZAC) and Remembrance Day commemorations in Australia and New Zealand. However, the journey of this documentary was fraught with an array of obstacles that tested each and every element of its research towards the later production as a television programme.

*Missing: Presumed Dead* was a gift, as was the chance discovery of the wallet. It was central to many elements of my life across that time, in terms of historical research (I was employed part-time at the Adelaide City Archives as the Curator of Civic Collections whilst I developed my business), unresolved familial history, entrepreneurial and intrapreneurial pursuits, and later as an element of my research that would lead to doctoral studies at the Entrepreneurship, Commercialisation, and Innovation Centre (ECIC) as part of the Faculty of Professions at the University of Adelaide.

I would travel across five countries to record interviews, and vision, with Vanna, whom I would marry in a service at Durham in England during the final days of our shoot (where I had been born on a return family visit by my parents after they had immigrated to Australia). Vanna and I left a memorable wedding lunch at Durham city to travel to Washington village to continue the shoot and record a very emotionally moving interview with the parents of my childhood friend Norman Dent. Norman had been killed whilst a Flight Lieutenant serving in the Royal Air Force (RAF) as a Navigator with 14 Squadron, in a Tornado combat strike aircraft in early 1991.

## Change Is Catalysed by Creativity and Its Intangibilities

Change is the constant we live with every second. It makes life possible. It also makes for purpose and the challenge of variety. It is the basis of our existence, and we deal with it as a practice of our lives as humans, and have done adaptively for millennia.

The very essence of change is creativity in relation to organic life. It is the intangible fuel that is at its source and often exists at the fringes of the perceived control points of human, natural and other societies as we move towards the next industrial age (Schwab 2016; Schwab and Davis 2018). It is at the seemingly uncontrolled edges that we advance socially, economically, politically, artistically, scientifically, towards all other modes of endeavour and enterprise. Yet, as detailed by Thomas Kuhn (1922–1996) (1970, 1977, 1996, 2011), these cyclical iterations are always in movement towards change, in terms of revolutionary cycles, often in the spiralling continuum. The *paradigm shift* is now commonly spoken of, and yet it was created and posited as potential by Thomas Kuhn, and is but an aspect of his cyclically iterative observations and philosophical proposition on what is termed the Kuhn Cycle (2012) as depicted in Fig. 1.8.

Change is with us. It is to be embraced and understood in terms of risk and the mitigation of potentially damaging aspects of it, as much as can be prepared for. Taking risks has been the mode of our learning as a species.

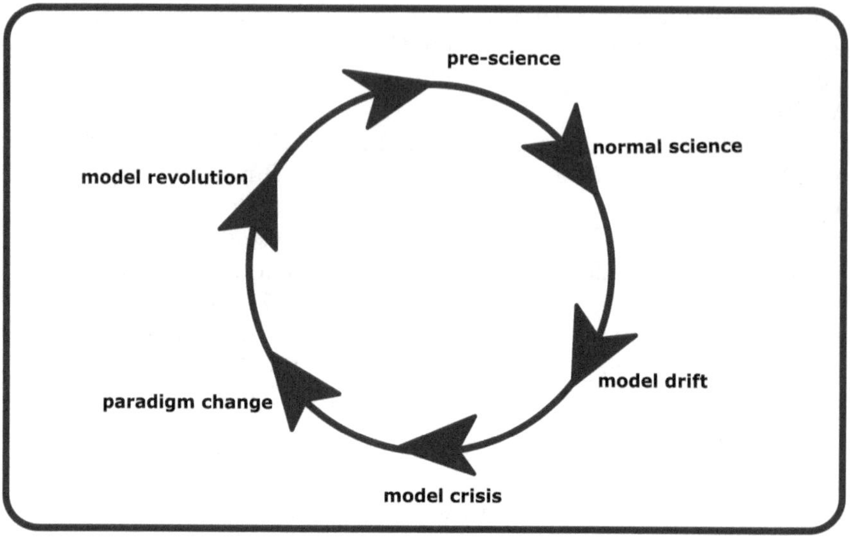


**Fig. 1.8** The Kuhn Cycle (Kuhn 1970, 1996, 2011; Pajares 2013; The Kuhn Cycle 2012). (Prepared by Author)

Each difference in mode or behaviour is tempered against the risk involved, and in some cases the risk is far too great to proceed, and therefore the change does not take place, or must desist. It is through risk that we as humans learned what to eat, or not. Berries, mushrooms, other foraging gains could be our sustenance or potentially our discontinuation. And here we are the inheritors of a past of risk-taking, and its amelioration.

Consider the remarkable construction and detail of the novel *Frankenstein* or *The Modern Prometheus* (1818, 1821) written by Mary (née Godwin) Wollstonecraft Shelley (1797–1851) about an augmented human, as a discussion point of morality and ethics; and the friendly rivalry of the writers at Lake Geneva where Mary Wollstonecraft Shelley (2014) derived a most remarkable and prophetic tale of a constructed life made animate.

At the location of Lake Geneva, where Maison Chapuis and Villa Diodati had been rented during the summer of 1816, the recounting of German ghost stories, and the circumstances of weather conditions led to the challenge to write a story which became the Gothically inspired apex of creativity of a remarkably inspired author. And yet all was contextual and inspired by the changes taking place in this era and which had been witnessed by Mary and others who discussed '18th Century natural philosopher and poet Erasmus Darwin who is said to have animated dead matter, ... and the feasibility of returning a corpse or assembled body parts to life' (Wollstonecraft Shelley 2014, p. 9).

## The Zeitgeist or Spirit of the Time, or Time Ghost

To set the scene and in the spirit of the zeitgeist, on Lake Geneva, during periods of inclement weather across a summer of tempestuous activity, the party discussed German ghost stories, prompting Lord George Gordon Byron (1788–1824) to propose they should all write a story of 'supernatural' dimensions. Mary Shelley, awaking from a dream, wrote a short story about a re-animated human, and encouraged by Percy Shelley (1792–1822) to continue to a novel, becoming her first, entitled *Frankenstein* or *The Modern Prometheus* published in 1818 (Wollstonecraft Shelley 2014).

When examining the genesis of an augmented human and the birth of artificial intelligence, this catalytic gathering would fuel the imaginations of future generations, and be the inspiration of a social and cultural inheritance that accepted it was possible. Countess Ada Lovelace (1815–1852) would grow up without her father, Lord Byron; however, she would be successful in deriving the first machine algorithm and anticipating a bug or computer virus. Not perhaps ready at this juncture to accept that artificial intelligence was possible, Countess Ada Lovelace nonetheless began an exponential incline that we are experiencing acutely in the emergent era of the Fourth Industrial Revolution.

## Waxing and Waning Moon

As humans and the societies we are formulating, whether local, national or global [to those off-Earth (OECD 2016) potentially], it can be seen that as a species we are in progression exponentially with developing technologies. In recent centuries, we have gone through industrial revolutions, being as distinct categories of innovation, steam, electricity, semiconductor and cyber-physical systems or quantum computing (Schwab 2016; Schwab and Davis 2018).

*Frankenstein* is pure innovation, however, holistically the result of Mary Wollstonecraft Shelley's experience with the Royal Society. And it hints at the electrical age, the use of electricity on human bodies as demonstrated in the context of science.

We augment film, and therefore reality. It is not necessarily reality, but a version of it, an augmented version. *Frankenstein,* being artificial intelligence, an example of an augmented human, commenced as a stream of consciousness, creativity and innovation for Mary Wollstonecraft Shelley (2014). It was then captured in a bound book, to later be represented as a linear projected narrative, in various contexts and with a variety of inclusions, and omissions, from the first conceived text, which importantly started as a short story.

## The Balsamic Moon and the Intangibles

In terms of a stream of conscious that we draw from when considering the perhaps indeterminant depths possible of intangibility, creativity and innovation is an integrated system of existence in all of us. I was introduced to the idea of the balsamic moon when I had my astrological chart read as a generous offer of exchange for an interview I provided to a film-maker (and astrologist) in Adelaide, during my early investigations into what I termed at the time, inherited grief (later termed contextually against DNA transformations resultant of epigenetic modifications), and which would become the essence and drive to complete the documentary *Missing: Presumed Dead.*

The balsamic moon is the zeitgeist of astrological interpretation, as I appreciate it, and enables those who are fortunate to have the alignment to be able to anticipate eventualities. At a very early stage during my adolescence, I learnt to trust instinct in all manner of pursuits, and in sometimes perilous circumstances. I have since investigated the gut instinct (Soosalu et al. 2019) as part of entrepreneurship and innovation; and a historical appraisal of the holistic nature of the brain beginning in the gut, which was known to Hippocrates (460–370 BCE), and has been rediscovered in a sense with neuro-scientific research that is propelling a range of potentialities in terms of bio-technological and cyber automaton technological applications across the Fourth Industrial Revolutionary (Schwab 2016; Schwab and Davis 2018) cycle, and its ever-expansive context of possibilities and potentialities (James Wilson and Daugherty 2018).

When Vanna, as co-founder, and I made a dedicated and concerted push to accelerate our start-up venture from South Australia nationally, and internationally, we utilised the *parabolic scramble* framework in our business endeavours, as it had emerged from my doctoral research study. It would enable us to bounce back effectively across the numerous projects we pursued with an ability to flexibly recalibrate our time, effort and resources to triage as required. We both embraced the unknown with a vigour and determination that had a range of results, and through which we both learnt the true cost of entrepreneurial endeavour, and the associated risks involved.

I was up for the roller-coaster ride and did the full journey cyclically, many times, until staggering off at the end to take a breather before being able to face it again, and would discuss these trials and tribulations often with Vanna, as we collectively got back on the ride, and prepared figuratively for the big dipper, and the loop, to the corkscrew. I would learn through the experience that this was typical of early start-ups, not all of course; however, most definitely the majority as the interviews that I conducted with Academic Director at ECIC, Dr Allan O'Connor, would starkly reveal as we conducted research into entrepreneurial ecosystems in South Australia (O'Connor and Reed 2014a, b, 2015a, b). I completed this research with Allan whilst finalising my doctoral studies at The University of Adelaide's specialist entrepreneurial faculty, ECIC, and as part of a report for the South Australia Department of State Development to effect entrepreneurial outcomes across local, national and global economic contexts.

Despite a balsamic moon in my astrological sphere, I was unaware of the true cost of entrepreneurial endeavour as it swept away a marriage, and by consequence a home, with all its constituent parts. However, life would, and did, go on remarkably, contrary to all my expectations. With all our resources, fiscal, physical and emotional, placed into the objective, there would be distinct successes in an intensively competitive fragmenting televisual market, though there was a high cost to the activity. For it seemed that in terms of the screen market at this time, as we advanced and seemingly made gains with our strategic, well-established screen production partners, and ground was figuratively taken, we were now well behind the new paradigm with its shift far to the forward.

As I recovered from this intense commercially testing start-up experience, I remembered keenly entrepreneurs I had interviewed, who had recounted their own profound and testing experiences in the crucible, and their tentative steps to return to entrepreneurial enterprise and endeavours afterwards, the legacy of such a *baptism of fire*.

Much like them, I tentatively returned after rebuilding a life. It is a changed life. Not one I in anyway regret. I learnt in the most extreme of circumstances, whether journeying through unknown territories and spaces or not, that my instincts could always be trusted, and my resolve and commitment of balance against the potential destruction of persistence. I was tested with profound risk, and survived to tell the tale, which I am now able to share with you, the reader.

## The Voyage into Intangibility

When embarking upon any journey towards a destination for the first time, there is often an idea, or imagined vision, of what it will be like on arrival. For the entrepreneur navigating the metaphysical space of an unknown universe, to potentially entrepreneurial ecosystem multiverses (O'Connor and Reed 2017) where there are variables and potentially a disrupted environment that requires constant adjustments and recalculations, this may seem impossible or at times incomprehensible. And yet, it is this very unknown universe, or multiverse, that the entrepreneur can become familiar with and navigate comfortably through its vastness, unpredictability and extremes.

We, as members of the human species, live with the unknown universe, or multiverse, every moment of our existence, as do other species on this planet, who thrive by trusting the impermanence of a largely intangible world.

Due to the limitations of our physiology, we are unable to see or comprehend 96 per cent of the universe, with the potential that it could be more than this. Through a deeper appreciation of theoretical physics in the final century of the last millennium came revelations provided by the cosmological constant regarding energy and matter, that notably made its originator, Albert Einstein (1879–1955), uncomfortable. A remarkably creative individual, who presented many qualities of entrepreneurial flair, Einstein's (1905, 1916, 1940) discoveries were so transformational that they disrupted his universe, that of contemporary scholars, and those of the past, present and future.

I propose that embracing the unknown is intrinsic and a daily reality for humans, and all creatures of this planet, throughout the stages of development; and for which we are collectively adept through our instincts, senses and comprehension of the seemingly incomprehensible.

When I was making my investigations to discover means by which an entrepreneur could interpret and understand their environment, I sought out economic models to interpret markets and frameworks to understand competitors; micro, meso, macro sectors; and modes of manufacturing, all of which assisted, however uniformly fell short of, the application I was seeking.

I realised I needed something quite specific to entrepreneurial endeavour early in my research journey, that I could use practically, and yet, it needed to embrace unique qualities, especially the variables of space and time. I also realised when searching for something specific, that trusting in the journey is key, going with the organic nature of our existence, by being in tune with our movement through space and time. The space and time that we negotiate every moment of the day was to be key, as we comprehend a moment and a day.

For what does this notion of a moment, or a day, really mean?

A moment was usually displayed on a timepiece, the minute hand on an analogue wristwatch or hall clock, or the frenetic digital display of an electronic representation of seconds, reductive potentially to milliseconds. The day itself being noted by the illumination of daylight, and by the lack of it. And yet, when I really think about the everyday nature of my physical movements on this planet, the true significance of my form in its context is revealed. My very existence is predicated on the fact that time is relative to my position on the geographical surface of a planet spinning on its axis, cycling through orbits predetermined by gravitational forces, largely conditional to the mass of other worlds, or astral bodies. All unseen, and though known to me, ethereally or perhaps even in vague terms, is largely irrelevant to my everyday existence as I cross the street from point A to B, or so it seemed. For this was my real journey, navigating the streets of the city I lived in at the time, a single human of the tens, hundreds, thousands, millions, billions of people who occupy this globe. The daily familiarity illuminated a pathway that would reveal itself when I chose to see things differently to how I had previously.

For the entrepreneur, seeing things differently is essential, if only by minute degrees, and trusting in that perception, even though it may be counter to current trends or established pathways. Trusting in the unknown or intangibles is a key starting point towards the creativity that will fuel innovative behaviours. The mitigation of risk is an important adjunct to the freedom of perception that the entrepreneur brings to the endeavour or enterprise, and if ascertained with clarity and judgement provides the safe environment in which to experiment. Much like crossing an intersection of roads, the movement from point A to B to C to D is a seemingly straightforward process and yet it is one that we are prepared for and become skilled in performing in order to safely negotiate variables of traffic, whether vehicular, pedestrian or other.

Much like being in the context of an intersection of roads and contemplating crossing it, the pedestrian is not necessarily contextualising their movement in terms of a global perspective, extending to a universe, or perhaps even, adventurously, a multiverse. No, the pedestrian focuses on the immediate action to achieve the goal, survive the dangers presented by the variables of traffic and successfully cross to the opposite side. To all intents and purposes, the micro is required here in order to survive the crossing with the meso, to macro perspective relevant as per the necessity and devices of the successful interaction and crossing of the juncture of pathways or roads.

For the entrepreneur, or intrapreneur, focusing on an objective or goal they may also not contemplate the broader perspective, or perhaps even realise that they are indeed being entrepreneurial or intrapreneurial. The definition of an entrepreneur or intrapreneur as what could be termed a profile is becoming revealed increasingly in all its variance and complexity to be multirole. When differing types of entrepreneurs began to be understood, there were terms formulated, such as builder, opportunist, specialist, innovator (Deeb 2014), and the list continues to grow upwards and outwards, as more is understood and researched. In its rich complexity is the combination of these types, with others to come potentially, nuanced against the requirements of the age, no doubt, and yet still to be revealed.

The creative practitioner, and in particular the screen creative practitioner for the purposes of this examination, otherwise known as a producer, is typically an entrepreneurial innovator, in a changing and disruptive global market for screen products, media enterprise and services or experiences potentially.

As humans made moon shots and JFK spoke of risk in space, and failure on the global scale of a Cold War engagement off-Earth, was he really in essence speaking of the notion of failure or the lack of such? If the USA was to succeed, it would be a great victory in the so-termed Space Race, and if not, it would be the unsuccessful attempt at a victorious outcome that could only be contextualised in the unique nature of the Cold War engagement where proxy was total.

When conceptualising the magnitude of the total warfare option of nuclear interchange, proxy was preferable, and if the contest was to be engaged off-Earth in the spirit of discovery and exploration, then so be it. It was monumental and yet, it could be argued inconsequential to the play of superpowers in the post-war nuclear age of science. And yet, in this contest of nationalistic governments extending their prestige through dominance over the planet's ruling systems of human-based structures, there was a commonality of humanity that was profound in its ambition. Both were ultimately successful in managing human survival in the vacuum of space. Perhaps it was this contest that made for a miraculous outcome and resultant of human beings walking on the moon's surface, for without the incremental successes that were planned for and tested systematically, there could be no landing of a vehicle on the lunar surface.

As National Aeronautics and Space Administration (NASA) prepared for success, they also mitigated for the lack of it, with pre-written statements mourning the loss of those individuals sent as ambassadors of humanity to another celestial body. Should the astronauts Neil Armstrong (1930–2012), Buzz Aldrin and Michael Collins (1930–2021), however, successfully journey to the fifth-largest natural planetary satellite in the solar system and return their historic venture would have profound consequences in its magnitude and scope, and be unifying for all nations on planet Earth.

It is an interesting reflection that a Cold War could be so productive in its achievements towards expansive goals of space exploration and a unity of humanity, given it was also a means to off-set potential Hot War engagement of cataclysmic proportions should there be a nuclear interchange on Earth, destroying humanity, or the majority of its populations and established cities, states, and national infrastructure. How often are the oppositional forces of such extremes so aligned to life and death, success and supposed failure, a yes and a no, a да или нет (da or a nyet), an Astronaut or a Космонавт (Cosmonaut), capitalism or communism? In such extremes, there was the competitive balance of effort towards a united goal or outcome, and as such when mapping this profound era of discovery, can be seen a unified human directive to break the bounds and bonds of our shared planet and venture into the expanse of a universe. Neil Armstrong symbolised humanity's accomplishment and stated it as such, the great achievement of divergent, convergent, risk, reward, innovation, entrepreneurial and intrapreneurial endeavour, an extension of the scientific method. All knowledge that humanity had derived across the millennia went into this combined effort, and the humans on planet Earth experienced the achievement collectively.

The universe could be indifferent to the subtleties of national identities, language and structures across geopolitical posturing, as in the vacuum of space all were equal in the terms of whether they were equipped to survive or not.

What can the entrepreneur or intrapreneur learn from the space programmes, or space race, in this era? Essentially, how to navigate the unknown incrementally by being prepared, having the right equipment, being systematic and safety conscious. Be bold and brave in the face of the unknown, or little known, by being prepared to seek knowledge and experience.

This book draws from the space programmes of last century, and this, with the advent of a new millennium, is the expansion of interest in space exploration through research and distinct action (OECD 2016). With many national governments seeking interests in space exploration, so too is the commercial sector venturing forth into the expanse of the unknown universe, albeit tentatively with incremental steps akin to earlier developments, with entrepreneurs leading the way on this new commercial frontier. The space race continues, just in a new format, for a new age has dawned in the expanse of space and our fledgling albeit tentative steps towards its further definition. We will in the future know more about the planetary systems of the expanding universe because in one form or another we are going to go there, whether as human explorers taking our life support systems and atmosphere with us, or by proxy of vehicular machines, robotic forms or other intelligences be it artificial or otherwise.

What the future holds is the unknown and as we embark upon the journey towards off-Earth exploration with the potential of settlement by humans or machines, we are Earth-bound; and, amidst the many global developments of the recent era, is the advent of the Fourth Industrial Revolution (Schwab 2016; Skilton and Hovsepian 2018). A defining period of technological and economic advancement noted by the end of one era, being the Third Industrial Revolution, and the commencement of the next, in a relatively succinct transition of time. As the Digital Revolution dove-tailed with the last noted Industrial Revolutionary cycle, so too did its antecedents prepare the fertile ground for the next, as an exponential climb across the vastness of a new space and time in the history of human societal development.

The disruption that has occurred was necessary to the distinct transition from the respective revolutionary cycles, and yet, as Thomas Kuhn described, his own Kuhn Cycle as seen in Fig. 1.9 was much more descriptive of the cycles of revolution that are taking place every day, throughout time and space, as we experience it incrementally. Noting that from

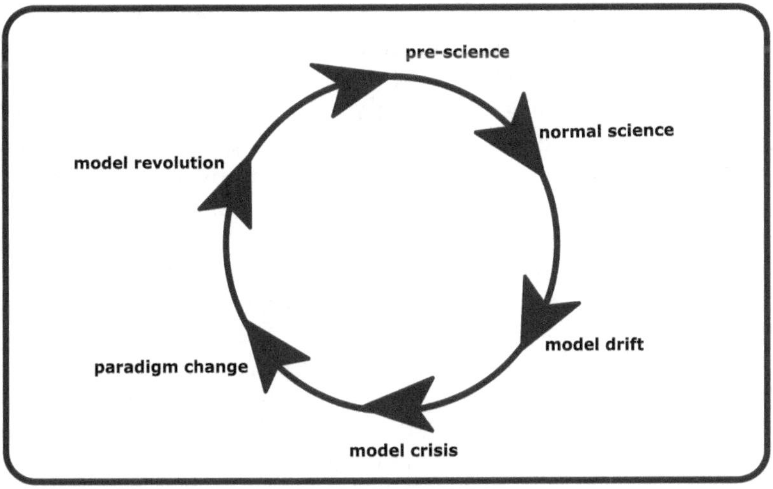


**Fig. 1.9** The Kuhn Cycle (Kuhn 1970, 1996, 2011; Pajares 2013; The Kuhn Cycle 2012). (Prepared by Author)

pre-science through the arc of normal science to model drift, and model crisis, there can be the appearance of no changes taking place at all. That is until the point of revolutionary change, which then transforms the paradigm towards the next iterative cycle.

Professor Tim Flannery outlines communication between plants and, in particular, trees, and these species' difference from humans in terms of time. A more than 9500-year-old spruce tree in Sweden (Wohlleben 2016) in comparison to humans is in excess of 115 lifespans, being approximately 82–83 years on average for the latter organisms.

Questioning time and space, in relation to the tree, and the universe, our time here on Earth is different elsewhere, as we are in tune with the cycles of our solar system. Day and night are determined by the Earth spinning on its axis, not the orbits of the sun and yet, those orbits affect the length of day and night, and influence the seasons of the year (a cycle of 365 days and 366 in a leap year).

For the entrepreneur and for the purposes of investigating the existent ecosystem for screen production, an exploratory company was utilised, and unexpectedly through the processes of the research was metaphorically compared to the Voyager probes launched by NASA. This movement to engage with the unknown, through the established device of a vehicle that is prepared, and sent on its mission is much akin to the entrepreneur, and the entrepreneurial endeavour embarked upon. For it is much assumed where such a journey will lead and yet, as evidenced by the Voyager probes, what was expected through the existent knowledge and experience based upon the parameters of Earth did not always translate to the planetary systems of our celestial neighbours, and as progression was made through space and the Milky Way Galaxy.

Inspirationally, with an open mind and heart, economist Edith Penrose (1914–1996) undertook research mid-last century, on commission, to evaluate the Hercules Powder Company (Penrose 1955, 1959) and assess its components of business. This was during the post-war era and there had been a lot of use for gunpowder, and despite the potential in this era for a resurgence in armed conflict, the market was inevitably changing, presenting potentialities that were in need of exploration. Famously Edith Penrose's discoveries were to be transformational to the way we, especially in the Discipline of Entrepreneurship, understand the notion of intangibles and intangibility. For someone, really anyone, venturing into the unknown, this is a comfort, and as an entrepreneur to understand that which is not presenting solid evidence is a test, a test of belief, of courage, and potentially faith. Personal belief needs to present itself as faith to the entrepreneur, bravely venturing into the unknown, armed with only a conviction, albeit based upon their judgement, experience, knowledge and sense of what is correct and right in terms of the pathway, though the tactics and strategy may be evolving.

As outlined earlier, with neuroscience we can now say with confidence that the entrepreneur's gut feel for what is correct is to be believed and trusted, because science and modern medicine have proven it to be so, even though Hippocrates knew it was so, as did the many who knew of the power of holistic approaches to body, mind and spirit. Edith Penrose was no different, trusting in the power of a new discovery, she was able to extend to elements of a business that could not be defined easily however were essential and present, just not necessarily in a physical form. They were as important as the bricks and mortar, or the means of production and yet, were not easily seen by the observer, for they were intangible.

There is a bravery attributed to those who venture where no person has been before. And perhaps we already have an inheritance from those who have existed before us that collectivises as a knowledge basis that exists and is there if we are open to receive its wisdom. Or perhaps it is a case of trusting the self-knowledge that we have, either intrinsically or as a development from our experiences throughout a remarkable existence that we have during a lifespan.

When we consider the spruce in Sweden, its lifespan is continuous across multiple human lifespans. It is our connection with a past, with an origin of 10,000 years. Imagine if we were to have that knowledge. Yet, in our own lifespan we do, for we are a continuum of the past to the present to the future, our past and the past experience of others, who have taught us, inspired us, instructed us. Theirs is a precious gift of knowledge that we either make our own or not; we pass on or we do not; we treasure or we do not; we see its true value or we do not see any value. It is for us to be open to the richness of the past and the experiences of others. It is there to be seen, if we have the eyes focused to see it clearly. We already know so much because we live it every day; we are practised and we perfect our practice; we are skilled and we hone our skills yet further. We intrinsically adapt and become adept at the modes of being in this world, of living on the planet's surface or being healthy in our environment or by not being so. We work to a goal every day, even if we at some stage feel ourselves to be directionless, our existence is testament to our vigour and nature; we are the continuum.

When we consume the story of space exploration, either as historical record or that which is conceived to be fictional, it is the truth with which our connection as humans is gauged to be legitimate. It is always our connection as genus homo that is the value. For the entrepreneur to initiate a series of events that result in the production of a product, service, experience, process or other, there is a connection to the empathic need of another being, the supply of something tangible or intangible that meets that need, want or desire or can address an opportunity. And, notably in its truest form, and when the entrepreneur has connected completely, the transaction is one of complete giving, for the entrepreneur has furnished a sentient being with something that makes their existence easier or more fulfilled.

The exploratory enterprise discovers and encounters new problems and issues as it travels into the unknown, akin to the Voyager Programme's exploratory probes (Spinks 2013), of market and processes that it innovatively interprets and negotiates.

The movement towards the exploration of space has been a distinct direction for our species genus homo, born of this planet, and yet also born in the solar system, the Milky Way Galaxy, in the greater context of an expanding universe, fuelled by the forces of the Big Bang as astrophysicists detail, and resultant of inflationary pressure. So, can we consider ourselves planetists, or solar systemists, galaxyists or universists? All new words, and according to my current spell check incorrect, which of course they possibly are, and yet in the Penrosian pioneering quest into the unknown, I am experimenting with the new, new words for new thoughts, and potentially a new identity beyond the bounds of geography, and a single language, here on Earth. One perhaps creates a new normal, and when this becomes the now normal, move to the post new normal, to ever expand the notion of normality, which, of course, can never be truly established, for all is changing constantly. It is just that we seek a conformity, or establishment, that is deemed to be 'normal'; however, it is simply the present moment in change.

As a way to achieve an exploration off-Earth and potentially a human presence in space, there needs to be considered the issue of a lifespan, as in many cases we may not be physically able to travel the distances required without expending the duration of our finite existence, and essentially running out of time and dying. There are several possibilities here, and in many ways, they are being prepared for now, in the true spirit of space innovation and its developments over the past several decades. The Voyager probes (Skilton and Hovsepian 2018), very much accelerators to the '... achieve[ments of] the 3rd Industrial [R]evolution ...' (p. 6), that ventured into the unknown and discovered phenomena never before conceived by their creators, continue the journey and will do so for potentially 40,000 years, equating to approximately 481.92 human lifespans at the average age of 83 years, and 4.02 spruce trees, referenced on the lifespan of 9950 years, as per the longest living tree located at Sweden. So, we have four options, we stay on Earth and do not venture into space; or we go, taking what we need in terms of human (and potentially non-human, Earth-based species), to sustain our organic format at the remarkable cost that represents, in terms of oxygen and water. Or we augment ourselves with requisite technologies, or, as has been done in recent decades, we send vehicles and robotic machines that are remotely controlled from an Earth-based locality.

As we have entered the Fourth Industrial Revolution with all its emerging technological promise, there is consideration of the position of machines in the future context of co-habitation with humans. Beyond a range of moral and ethical considerations is the notion of empowered artificial intelligent, also known as AI, formats that through machine learning (ML) will quickly advance beyond the intellectual and physical limits of humanity and then seek to dominate, and potentially enslave organic beings. In the more extreme representation, the organic format may be rendered obsolete but AI will illuminate its presence on Earth, and potentially elsewhere. However, beyond the notion, or depictions in popular fiction, of a dystopian future of humans in bunkers engaged in conflict scenarios with machines, is a balanced integration whereby there is no malice, and fear is not a factor. It is the complement of human and machine, a true partnership in terms of augmentation, which may transpire to increasingly be the embedding of technology in our own structure, to replace, enhance and extend the capacity and longevity of the human form. Essentially, human beings and AI sources will exist in tandem or in a format of collaboration (James Wilson and Daugherty 2018) as it does so already in contemporaneous human society, and will exponentially grow as a symbiosis.

## The Exploratory Company as an Enterprise of Discovery

The use of an exploratory company as an enterprise and effective vehicle of data collection in a context of discovery was remarkably productive, and in its own format versatile. By taking the exploratory company completely out of the screen sector, the search for other forms and formats could begin. It was to be a rich and empowering journey. Much akin to what NASA discovered with its Voyager probes, it was often unexpected and not possible to conceive from an Earth-based perspective, and, in the case of the exploratory company, a screen-based perspective. It was immersive and reductive, although existent in a fragmenting and expanding market, not dissimilar to the expanding nature of the universe that the Voyager probes were launched into and continue to explore.

As Franklin Delano Roosevelt (1882–1945) (FDR) famously said during his inaugural address, when he foresaw the economic struggle ahead as he sought to initiate the reconstruction of an economy laid waste by The Great Depression, 'all we have to fear is fear itself'. FDR and JFK had the ability to mobilise a people through eloquence and demonstrated leadership during periods of colossal challenge. They were inspirational. In both cases, these leaders were dealing with the unknown, a future without definition, except for the future that would be created, and which they would lead their constituents towards, with bravery and fearlessness.

A framework entitled the *parabolic scramble* is emergent from the embedded research, and this discovery transforms all aspects of the exploratory company's interactions with local and global markets, and importantly across all aspects of its operational and strategic processes.

Whilst conducting research and immersed in its discoveries, I had a fortuitous revelation of the processes of a scramble or diagonal crossing (Barnes 1965) in the City of Adelaide, South Australia. The recently introduced scramble crossing was unknown to most of its users, who were now free to move anywhere within the bounded area of the intersection of roads; as a pedestrian, you could choose your own path. And yet, the established linear movement was adopted by the pedestrians, as can be seen in Fig. 1.10, and remained the norm for the initial period of my own interactions, where I too adopted a path of dependency, assuming that it

**Fig. 1.10** Scramble crossing, King William Street intersecting Waymouth and Pirie Streets in the City of Adelaide. (Photograph by Author)

was the most efficient course of action because it was in a straight line. In reality, the pathway was congested and when the two diagonal pathways met in the centre of the intersection of roads, there was congestion and the movement of the pedestrians slowed, or became chaotic.

I would cross the intersection of roads a number of times until the day when I adopted a seemingly instinctive parabolic curvature as I left the kerb to cross diagonally between the opposing pavements of the intersection of roads. This parabolic curvature meant that I was uninterrupted in my passage through the scramble crossing. I was free to interpret my own pathway, and as I walked I missed any congestion and arrived at my intended destination before any other pedestrians had crossed the intersection. The parabolic curve had proved to be the most efficient interpretation and action in the scramble crossing to enable me to quickly cross it.

The scramble crossing has been introduced to cities where there is a high pedestrian concentration in the intersection because it is efficient. However, if pedestrian numbers are low, it is not as efficient, and there are a range of considerations regarding the time it takes to cross the intersection of roads, as a pedestrian, with the requisite pressure this places on the vehicular traffic and associated arterial road infrastructures. A simple crossing of the road, which I had done every day, in some cases several times in that city, was to be a revelation to my thinking and processes.

I began to experiment, as can be seen in its early stages in Fig. 1.11, with it as a metaphor for entrepreneurial endeavour, where a different pathway is needed, and an observance of path dependency is important. Not to say that under certain circumstances the path of dependency is not relevant, or redundant, for it may be the most efficient and proven mode of interaction.

There were also to be the interesting observed developments. One evening, a car moved through the scramble crossing unexpectedly, to the great surprise of the pedestrians. The vehicle's driver had misread the traffic signals, possibly because it was night and the environment perhaps not familiar. Disaster was averted that evening due to low numbers in the scramble crossing. However, it was a stark example of how we view an environment and the actors within its bounds.

Another interesting and somewhat unusual event was when the entire state of South Australia lost its electrical power during a weather event. The police officer as depicted in Figs. 1.12a and 1.12b manually instituted the conditions of the scramble crossing with great skill and ease. Pedestrians and vehicles alike behaved as though the crossing were equipped with its

**Fig. 1.11** Notebook entries documenting the *parabolic scramble* and its potential utility. (Photograph and drawing by Author)

power sources. In a sense it was, just in a different format, and down to one person, and actors who most likely knew their role well as participants in the bounded area of the scramble crossing.

The Penrosian discovery of intangible assets appeared key to many aspects of the unknown, as demonstrated by Albert Einstein who impressively conceived relativity whilst working in the Swiss Patent Office in Bern to Karl Schwarzchild (1873–1916) who proved it, whilst serving in the German army in the trenches of WWI, later succumbing to an autoimmune disorder, initiated by the conditions of the conflict. Remarkable

**Fig. 1.12a** A police officer orchestrating the scramble crossing. (Photograph by Author)

**Fig. 1.12b** A police officer orchestrating the scramble crossing. (Photograph by Author)

creatives, operating in the early decades of last century with a transformational impact upon that century, all based upon intangibility, because you couldn't place the universe in a laboratory and test it.

When Albert Einstein discovered the universe was expanding, as noted earlier, he wanted to put his cosmological constant back into the bottle. However, it was out, and would never really be able to be contained again. Even though Einstein wished to conform to his contemporaries, it would not be possible. Nor could the cosmological constant be contained in terms of its profound revelations of energy and matter, and the intangibility of the universe for the human, who notably and remarkably cannot see the 96 per cent of it. Penrosian intangibility would be further developed in the Discipline of Entrepreneurship, importantly by academic Professor Jay Barney (1991), with incorporated elements in the resource-based view (RBV) of the firm (Kor and Mahoney 2004; Mahoney and Pandian 1992).

The exploratory company is able to build upon and reflexively interpret changing market landscapes and adjust with an agility of purpose and application that are unique, and for others in the market, potentially transferrable.

Preparing to engage in the screen sector and its markets nationally and internationally, as it fragmented and began to become complex was an increasing challenge for the new company, especially as resources began to be stretched both fiscally and through the finite labours of its co-founders. The number of projects needed to be viable was on a ratio of ten to one, as detailed by the market. Interaction with established companies meant that the new company began to partner with others to gain commercial experience, traction and credibility with the market. They were in the main broadcasters across the public and private sectors, as well as established production companies with national and international reach.

The *parabolic scramble* was used by the co-founders to adjust to the changing market and be agile in their dealings with broadcasters and the need to quickly re-direct resources to or away from a project, whether in conceptual, pre-development, development or moving to production phases.

For the entrepreneur, or those yet to be, through using the framework of the *parabolic scramble*, they are able to prepare for and develop through phases of unknown encounters, where incremental adjustments are translated back into the organisation and enable it to remain at the cusp of change in the market.

In dealing with phases that presented in terms of unknown occurrences, or encounters in the market, the *parabolic scramble* gave the co-founders a framework that began to inform the creation of strategy, culture, approaches to projects and markets, decision making and a range of unforeseen issues, positive or negative in terms of impact. The main benefit was that the *parabolic scramble* enabled the important incremental adjustments needed to be fed back into the organisation in order to retain an ability to react and respond to changes in the market almost instantly, as they presented and became known and evident. The inculcation of the initial metaphor of the *parabolic scramble* to something that could be used as an intangible positive force in the company was almost indescribable due to the nature of its embeddedness and the means by which it had been generated as part of the company's development.

As the company ventured further into the unknown universe of disruption in an ever-expanding fragmenting environment of space, it was the *parabolic scramble* that became its vehicle to uncover and deal with the intangibles it encountered in an inflationary and therefore ever-complex emergent universe of opportunity. In summary, the *parabolic scramble* was the means by which the entrepreneurs could navigate the fragmenting and disrupted areas that they needed to traverse and be at ease with.

So, had begun the voyage into intangibility, which for the entrepreneur is a space that is to be a comfort, for if you are not in that space, you are not navigating the disruption needed to traverse the universe, known, unknown and yet-to-be discovered.

## Bibliography


Alexander C. 2003. *The Bounty*. London: Harper Collins Publishers.

Barnes HA. 1965. *The Man with the Red and Green Eyes: The Autobiography of Henry A. Barnes, Traffic Commissioner, New York City*. New York: E P Dutton & Co.

Barney J. 1991. "Firm Resources and Sustained Competitive Advantage." *Journal of Management* 17, no. 1: 99–120.

Blank S. 2013. "Why the Lean Start-up Changes Everything." *Harvard Business Review*. https://hbr.org/2013/05/why-the-lean-start-up-changes-everything.

Blank S. 2018. *NewTV is the Antithesis of a Lean Startup. Can it work?* https://hbr.org/2018/08/newtv-is-the-antithesis-of-a-lean-startup-can-it-work.

Bligh, W, Bach J, National Library of Australia. 1987. The Bligh Notebook: "Rough account – Lieutenant Wm Bligh's voyage in the Bounty's launch from the ship to Tofua & from thence to Timor", 28 April to 14 June 1789, with a draft list of the Bounty mutineers. Canberra: National Library of Australia.

Burchett W. 1977. *Grasshoppers & Elephants: Why Viet Nam Fell.* Urizen Books, Collingwood.

Cooper B, Vlaskovits, P. 2016. *The Lean Entrepreneur: How Visionaries Create Products, Innovate with New Ventures, and Disrupt Markets.* New York: Wiley & Sons.

Csikszentmihalyi M. 1999. "Implications of a Systems Perspective for the Study of Creativity" In R. J. Sternberg (ed.). *Handbook of Creativity.* Cambridge: Cambridge University Press: 313–35.

Csikszentmihalyi M. 2004. "Flow, the Secret to Happiness." Ted Talk. https://www.ted.com/talks/mihaly_csikszentmihalyi_on_flow?language=en#t-918.

Daly P. 2013. "Towards a City of Entrepreneurs: The Emergence of Adelaide as a Recognised Start-up Community." Paper presented at the Towards a City of Entrepreneurs forum, Adelaide Convention Centre, 25 June.

De Bono E. 1992. *Serious Creativity: Using the Power of Lateral Thinking to Create New Ideas.* London: Harper Collins Business. Imprint of Harper Collins Publisher.

De Bono E. 2016. *Parallel Thinking.* London: Penguin Books.

Deeb G. 2014. "The 4 Types of Entrepreneurs–Which Are You?" *Forbes Online.* https://www.forbes.com/sites/georgedeeb/2014/11/07/the-4-types-of-entrepreneurs-which-type-are-you/ - 3f03fc153e9e

Design Council. 2019. *The Design Process: What is the Double Diamond*?https://www.designcouncil.org.uk/news-opinion/design-process-what-double-diamond.

Einstein A. 1905. "Eine neue Bestimmung der Molecküldimensionen." PhD Thesis. Universität Zürich, Zürich. http://www.pitt.edu/~jdnorton/lectures/Rotman_Summer_School_2013/Einstein_1905_docs/Einstein_Dissertation_German.pdf

Einstein A. 1916. Die Grundlage der Allgemeinen Relativitätstheorie. Annalen Der Physik. Vierte Folge (Fourth Episode). *Band* 49, no. 7: 770–822. http://www.physik.uni-augsburg.de/annalen/history/einstein-papers/1916_49_769-822.pdf.

Einstein A. 1940. "Science and Religion." *Nature* 146, no. 3706: 605–607.

Evatt H. 1955. *Rum Rebellion.* Sydney: Angus & Robertson.

Frederick H, O'Connor A, Kuratko, DF. 2019. *Entrepreneurship: Theory, Process, Practice.* 5th Asia-Pacific ed. Melbourne: Cengage Learning Australia.

Gammage B. 1974. *The Broken Years: Australians in the Great War.* Canberra: ANU Press.

Gleeson B. 2018. "9 Navy Seal Sayings That Will Improve Engagement and Accountability in Your Organisation." *Forbes.* https://www.forbes.com/sites/

brentgleeson/2018/07/11/9-navy-seal-sayings-that-will-improve-engagement-and-accountability-in-your-organization/ - 22ab8b4e6312

Hough R. 1994. *Captain James Cook: A Biography.* London: Hodder and Stoughton Ltd.

James Wilson H, Daugherty P R. 2018. "Collaborative Intelligence: Humans and AI are Joining Forces." Boston: Harvard Business Review.

Kor Y, Mahoney J. 2004. "Edith Penrose's (1959) Contributions to the Resource-based View of Strategic Management." *Journal of Management Studies* 41, no. 1: 183–191.

Kuhn TS. 1970. *The Structure of Scientific Revolutions.* 2nd ed. Chicago: The University of Chicago Press.

Kuhn TS. 1977. "Objectivity, Value Judgement, and Theory Choice." Reprinted by permission from *The Essential Tension: Selected Studies in the Scientific Tradition and Change.* The University of Chicago Press, Chicago: 356–367. http://www.andrew.cmu.edu/user/kk3n/philsciclass/kuhn.pdf.

Kuhn TS. 1996. *The Structure of Scientific Revolutions.* 3rd ed. Chicago: The University of Chicago Press.

Kuhn TS. 2011. *Stanford Encyclopedia of Philosophy.* http://plato.stanford.edu/entries/thomas-kuhn/.

Levin G. 2013. "Jackson Pollock, Lee Krasner and a New Concept of Nature." *Ritsumeikan Studies in Language and Culture* 24, no. 3: 29–37.

Mahoney J, Pandian J. 1992. "The Resource-based View Within the Conversation of Strategic Management." *Strategic Management Journal* 13, no. 5: 363–380.

Mandelbrot B. 1977. *Fractals: Form. Chance and Dimension.* New York: W H Freeman and Company.

Mandelbrot B. 1982. *The Fractal Geometry of Nature.* New York: W H Freeman and Company.

Meagher RE. 2014. *Killing from the Inside Out: Moral Injury and Just War.* Oregon: Cascade Books.

O'Connor A, Reed GA. 2014a. *Innovating for Entrepreneurship in a Regional Milieu/Ecosystem: The Role of the University Sector.* Transatlantic Policy Consortium Conference. Indiana Memorial Union (IMU). Bloomington, 23–24 June.

O'Connor A, Reed GA. 2014b. *Adelaide Entrepreneurial Ecosystem: Policy Design and Program Research Grant Preliminary Report.* South Australia Department of State Development. Government of South Australia, Adelaide.

O'Connor A, Reed GA. 2015a. *Promoting Regional Entrepreneurship Ecosystems: The Role of the University Sector in Australia.* Australian Centre for Entrepreneurship Research Exchange (ACERE). The University of Adelaide, Adelaide, 3–6 February.

O'Connor A, Reed GA. 2015b. *South Australia's Entrepreneurial Ecosystem: Voice of the Customer Research Report.* South Australia Department of State Development. Government of South Australia, Adelaide.

O'Connor A, Reed GA. 2017. *From Helices to Multiverse Theory: Exploring the Diversity Within Entrepreneurial Ecosystems.* University Industry Innovation Network (UIIN). University Industry Engagement – International Asia-Pacific Conference. The University of Adelaide, Adelaide, 15–17 February.

OECD. 2016. *Space and Innovation.* Paris: OECD Publishing. https://doi.org/10.1787/9789264264014-en.

Pajares F. 2013. *The Structure of Scientific Revolutions: Outline and Study Guide.* Emory University. http://www.uky.edu/~eushe2/Pajares/Kuhn.html

Penrose E. 1955. "Research on the Business Firms: Limits to Growth and Size of Firms." *American Economic Review* 45, no. 2: 531–543.

Penrose E. 1959. *The Theory of the Growth of the Firm.* New York: John Wiley & Sons.

Reed GSW. 1998. "A Case Study into the Failure of the Team Concept at a Medium Sized Company and What Might be Done to Re-introduce It." Minor Thesis, Master of Total Quality Management (Honours), University of Wollongong.

Ries E. 2011. *The Lean Startup: How Today's Entrepreneurs Use Continuous Innovation to Create Radically Successful Businesses.* New York: Random House.

Sarasvathy SD, Venkataraman S. 2011. "Entrepreneurship as Method: Open Questions for an Entrepreneurial Future." *Entrepreneurship Theory and Practice* 35, no. 1: 113–135.

Schwab K. 2016. *The Fourth Industrial Revolution.* New York: Random House.

Schwab K, Davis N. 2018. *Shaping the Future of the Fourth Industrial Revolution.* New York: Crown Publishing Group.

Screen Australia. 2015a. *Hours of Australian Documentaries (Not Including Broadcaster-produced Titles) by Location of Production Company, 1997/98–2013/14.* Australian Government Screen Australia. https://www.screenaustralia.gov.au/fact-finders/production-trends/documentary-production/activity-summary

Screen Australia. 2015b. *Hours of First-Release Australian Documentaries Broadcast on Free-to-Air TV, 1998–2014*, Australian Government Screen Australia. http://www.screenaustralia.gov.au/research/statistics/releasesdocumentariestv.aspx.

Skilton M, Hovsepian F. 2018. *The 4th Industrial Revolution: Responding to the Impact of Artificial Intelligence on Business.* Cham: Palgrave Macmillan.

Sledge EB. 1981. *With the Old Breed: At Peleliu and Okinawa.* New York: Ballantine Books.

Soosalu G, Henwood S, Deo A. 2019. *Head, Heart, and Gut in Decision Making: Development of a Multiple Brain Preference Questionnaire*. SAGE Open. https://journals.sagepub.com/doi/full/10.1177/2158244019837439#articleCitationDownloadContainer

Spinks P. 2013. Voyager 1 Crosses the Final Frontier. *The Sydney Morning Herald*. http://www.smh.com.au/technology/sci-tech/voyager-1-crosses-the-final-frontier-20130913-2tpe2.html.

Steve Jobs Stanford Commencement Address. 2005. Stanford University, California, 14 June. http://news.stanford.edu/2005/06/14/jobs-061505/

Taylor R, Micolich P, Jonas D. 1999. *Can science be Used to Further Our Understanding of Art?* University of New South Wales. Physics World. October. http://authenticationinart.org/pdf/literature/Fractal-Expressionisme-Can-Science-Be-Used-To-Further-Our-Understanding-Of-Art.docx.pdf

The Kuhn Cycle. 2012. *Thwink.org*. http://www.thwink.org/sustain/glossary/KuhnCycle.htm

*The Vietnam War. 20*17. Television program. Volume one (episodes 1–5) Volume two (episodes 6–10) PBS Distribution.

Thompson J, Thompson S. 2018. *The Kremlinologist: Llewellyn E Thompson, America's Man in Cold War Moscow*. Baltimore: John Hopkins University Press.

Toyota. 2020. *Toyota Production System*. Toyota Motor Corporation. https://global.toyota/en/company/vision-and-philosophy/production-system/

Voss V. 1977. *Flying Minnows*. London: Arms & Armour Press.

Wohlleben P. 2016. *The Hidden Life of Trees: What They feel, How they Communicate – Discoveries From a Secret World*. Carlton: Black Inc.

Wollstonecraft Shelley M. 2014. *Frankenstein*. New York: Millennium Publications.

WWF Global. 2013. *Impact of Habitat Loss of Species*. World Wildlife Fund Global. https://wwf.panda.org/discover/our_focus/wildlife_practice/problems/habitat_loss_degradation/

CHAPTER 2

# Establishing the Means to Navigate the Unknown

When I consider my friend and mentor, Dennis, and his subtle direction, as my new company ventured into the unknown, I realise that, although he passed away during this time, he remained a constant guiding presence. As I ventured into the expanse of the universe and its unpredictability, especially across the Voyager probes and their inter-stellar investigations, Dennis was always there in spirit, urging me on, as he was embedded in my quest, a point of reference that I often referred to, either in the notes I recorded or the memory of his guidance.

Perhaps we are the product of all that we encounter in the universe at the moment in which we encounter mass and energy, and there is a cosmic overhang that results, or the connection is eternal. At the funeral service that concluded Dennis' life in its formal gathering and offering of testament to the character and importance of this individual were said the words that have lived with me, since that time.

Upon reflection, the religious service celebrating Dr Dennis List's life provided a profound statement and means of encapsulating the tangible and intangible (Barney 2001; Penrose and Pitelis 2009). It also provided a way to understand variables (Gleick 1987; Lorenz 1972; Mandelbrot 1977, 1982; Nash 1950a, b, 1951) and conceptual and methodological (Glaser and Strauss 1967, 28–31 and 40; List 2002, 2005; Reason and Bradbury 2008; Revans 1980, 1983; Shank 2006) exploration which has been so much a part of my endeavours throughout my life, and is a tribute



G. A. Reed, *Entrepreneurs Navigating a Universe of Disruption*,
https://doi.org/10.1007/978-981-19-0703-6_2

to Dennis and his legacy '... what is seen is transitory, what is unseen is eternal' (2 Corinthians 4:14–5:1).

When the Prime Minister of Britain, Mr Winston Spencer Churchill (1874–1965), contemplated walking with destiny, he was also contemplative of his advanced years and loss of the supposed youthful energy that could see him successfully engage with the monumental struggle ahead for the free world, as so deemed from the perspective of Britain in 1940 during what would become known as the Phoney War. And yet, if time is considered as rational to the progression of the statesperson gaining the experience needed to lead a nation, or any organisation, it must be through life and the living of it that this is achieved, with all its peaks and troughs, challenging and potentially destructive life events.

These are the prerequisites to the character development necessary to be robust in the face of adversity, not just advancing years. For it was Winston Churchill's experience and strength of character when pitted against adversity that could present eloquent reflection '... success is not final. Failure is not fatal. It is the courage to continue that counts' (*The Darkest Hour* 2017). A stirring and impactful notion, and quite possibly the words of Abraham Lincoln (1809–1865), as attribution is scant due to provenance of Churchillian sources, publicly and otherwise. Regardless, the modern essence of Winston Churchill and his legacy are inspirational, the persistence, tenacity and courage against great obstacles, both emotionally and physically.

It may be the case that Winston Churchill has received greater status in the decades following the victory of the 1939–1945 war, and his recovery from losing the general election of 1945, to which he expressed the sentiments of disappointment at not being wanted by the electorate after all he had done during the war years. And yet, Winston Churchill made some of his greatest speeches post-war in the five-year hiatus before his successful re-election to the British Parliament, as he toured the USA and re-orientated his focus to the challenge of the Cold War and the alignment and non-alignment of unambiguous *super-power* states.

It is the stirrings against struggle and adversity that Winston Churchill is now contextualised, and rightly so for he led a successful war cabinet towards a unified war effort, with his line of power defined. Perhaps this was his walk with destiny, and now our inspiration, for the leader did emerge. Where we draw strength is for us to determine. If it be in re-drafting the essence of the past, then so be it, or are we really the author of our success or otherwise? For it was Winston Churchill who stated,

'... For my part I consider it will be found much better by all Parties to leave the past to history, especially as I propose to write that history...' (DeadlineDetroit 2019), in that confidence of spirit from this Nobel Laureate (1963) who was born prematurely in circumstances that he remarkably recovered from, including delayed learning. We now know this can be a result of premature birth, but this was not known by his educators at St. Georges School, Brunswick School and later Harrow, or his father who expressed bitter disappointment with his son's scholastic achievements.

We too, in the spirit of Winston Churchill, are the authors of our destiny, whether all that is written about Churchill is accurate is perhaps not the point, for it is the essence of struggle against adversity which is to be admired and is inspirational. Winston Churchill was born of privilege and yet he was disadvantaged in his own context, a disadvantage regarding excellence that he struggled against to the point of a depressive state from which he incrementally recovered. It is the human element, and essence of this story that is the real inspiration, to continue by incorporating adversity and its lessons, to try to learn from the successes, near successes, and the distance that places the voyager at great peril, or not, in the pursuit of that success.

The *parabolic scramble* is based upon a diagonal pedestrian crossing typical of high-density areas of large, urbanised environments where vehicular and pedestrian traffic intersect at a point of regulated crossflows.

When contemplating the universe and its expansive, inflationary nature, there is a point at its very genesis towards singularity, or zero gravity, that is termed a scramble. I was drawn to this point when investigating entrepreneurial time, revealed during a journal writing exercise in an Enterprise Innovation class I was delivering at Surry Hills in Sydney, Australia. The subconscious is a wonderful companion, and this central feature in the universe was seemingly an accompaniment to my earlier discovery of the *parabolic scramble* framework based upon the diagonal crossing in Adelaide, 1372.7 kilometres away from my exact position when writing this text. Notable because time, speed, distance, velocity, mass, all have their intrinsic part to play and yet, as I write the text or utilise the *parabolic scramble* in the scramble crossing, how do I consider the speed at which I am traversing on the rotational axes of the planet and orbits around the sun?

I largely do not consider this at all, for it is largely irrelevant to my current circumstances. However, much like the night when a car entered the scramble crossing, as I was traversing an exclusive pedestrian zone, so too would a meteor hitting my current position on the globe be a seemingly unusual and risk-laden occurrence, for which I am accepting of in theory, or philosophically, and yet in reality am completely unprepared for.

Building upon the *parabolic scramble* is its augmentation through the use of technology, applying its utility for entrepreneurs, and those wishing to enter the entrepreneurial arena.

When considering the augmentation of reality and its associated technologies, it is vast in its promise and potential, and yet it is unknown to a large extent how augmented reality (AR) will find its place in the Fourth Industrial Revolution. There is speculation as to where AR will land commercially and practically across human society and its technologies. Being a sub-set of computer mediated reality (CMR), it is likely it will conjoin with virtual reality (VR) and in combination become mixed reality (MR), but this is undefined at this point. The unknown of CMR is a speculative environment where there is immense potential which is rich in its promise, and yet still vacuous in its deliverables. There will be incremental advances, and perhaps transformational at certain stages. At present, it is applied to a range of consumables from Pokémon Go apps to Living Wine Labels, though there are interesting applications in aviation and other fields which are showing distinct uptake.

It may be possible to assume that there is always a competitor who will perform at a higher capacity, whether at a sports' arena, market or global environment, and yet, is this really the case? It is the context that is important, and it is what is done with the *talents* that is important and ultimately unique. It is the combination of factors, including the complement of strengths that can propel a person or business entity or offering with a unique sense of self and application.

Augmentation of reality can be said to take place in many different contexts, such as the assembly of a narrative film, where in the early stages of film editing, the pieces of footage are cut and spliced together. The narrative that was formed was the beginning of screen language, or visual language, and developed its unique style with incremental improvements through the introduction of technology. The Éclair camera and its mobility allowed French filmmakers to make *cinéma vérité*, a style of gritty observational documentary building upon the Italian neo-realists of the post-war era in the mid-twentieth century from *Rome, Open City* (1945) (Roma Città Aperta) by Roberto Rossellini to *The Bicycle Thieves/The Bicycle Thief* (1948) (Ladri di biciclette) by Vittorio De Sica.

I have contextualised the augmentation of reality that has been the domain of creative producers, or screen producers, since the inception of the short-, medium- and long-form film product. These were produced by people to explain an augmentation of a reality, a story, a tale, a quest, a journey, a voyage and often sold as an experience on a screen, and later in custom-built cinemas. Two pieces of cellulose nitrate were joined together in Robert W. Paul's 1 minute 38 second comedy *Come Along, Do!* (1898) moving from the single-camera position to augment and entertain.

NASA Jet Propulsion Laboratory (JPL), California Institute of Technology, Pathfinder rover 'Sojourner' 1996–1997 landing on Ares Vallis on 4 July 1997 as depicted in Fig. 2.1. Two decades plus later, the descendant vehicle, NASA Mars Curiosity rover, as a true contemporary of the updated modern era, is captured on the surface of Mars by a panorama of images as depicted in Fig. 2.2. The automated nature of space exploration began decades ago, and now we have Earth-based remote-controlled vehicles exploring, photographing, taking samples of the surface and mapping it.

When Alex Kipman demonstrated Oculus Rift with a colleague across the road on Manhattan Island, New York, holographically, he did so with a to-scale depiction of the surface of Mars. The three holograms on stage conjoined to deliver a remarkable display, an exposition of the modern usage of holographic technology, as discovered by Dr Dennis Gabor (1900–1979) in 1947. The world has moved on, and we now explore planets with robotic devices delivered through the remotely controlled drones of spacecraft, and soon to be the exploratory drones that fly over the surface of atmospheric planetary environments across the solar system, galaxy and universe.

Change can be inspirational, such as George Bernard Shaw (1856–1950) describes, 'Progress is impossible without change and those that cannot change their minds cannot change anything'; and as Winston Churchill would state in the Commons on 23 June 1925, 'To improve is to change, so to be perfect is to have changed often'. In recent writings about the convergence of lean manufacturing towards the lean entrepreneur, Cooper and Vlaskovits (2016) and Ries (2011) devised ways to eliminate waste. Japan eliminated waste across their manufacturing processes late in the penultimate decade of the last millennium, to be refined in time for the new millennium. As a process for the Fourth Industrial Revolution, leanness now feeds into the entrepreneurial engine.

To build further on the suggestion that entrepreneurship will be as important as the scientific method for the next iteration of Industrial Revolution as made by Sarasvathy and Venkataraman (2011). In drawing a comparison with the early era where Francis Bacon defined a method of scientific enquiry, the authors suggest this importantly preceded the

**Fig. 2.1** 'Photojournal note: Sojourner spent 83 days of a planned seven-day mission exploring the Martian terrain, acquiring images, and taking chemical, atmospheric and other measurements. The final data transmission received from Pathfinder was at 10:23 UTC on September 27, 1997. Although mission managers tried to restore full communications during the following five months, the successful mission was terminated on March 10, 1998'. (Image Credit NASA/JPL)

**Fig. 2.2** 'A selfie taken by NASA's Curiosity Mars rover on Sol 2291 (January 15, 2019) at the "Rock Hall" drill site, located on Vera Rubin Ridge. This was Curiosity's 19th drill site. The drill hole is visible to the rover's lower-left; the entire scene is slightly dustier than usual due to a regional dust storm affecting the area. The selfie is composed of 57 individual images taken by the rover's Mars Hand Lens Imager (MAHLI), a camera on the end of the rover's robotic arm. The images are then stitched together into a panorama. MAHLI was built by Malin Space Science Systems, San Diego. NASA's Jet Propulsion Laboratory, a division of Caltech in Pasadena, manages the Mars Science Laboratory Project for the NASA Science Mission Directorate, Washington. JPL designed and built the project's Curiosity rover'. (Image credit: NASA/JPL-Caltech/MSSS)

implementation of the scientific method, and in essence provided the engine for the Industrial Revolution to occur. A methodology of testing hypotheses that has proved to be a great tool of the modern era, and made prolific in a global context that has produced exponential growth in terms of the creation of solutions to problems, and the equipping of genus homo with an array of options for its adaptive processes, both on and off-Earth as humanity ventures into the unknown expanse of space. Humans are investigating this space both experientially through selected individuals whose organic structures are supported with a transported Earthly environment, whether in a craft or suit, and then the drones, or robotic representatives as depicted in Figs. 2.1 and 2.2.

The remarkable nature of Earth meets the remarkable nature of a universe that is expansive and seemingly devoid of nature as humans know it, and yet it is also natural. The universality of nature is within us all, and throughout all creation, for it is a creation that we are part of, and it is part of us. We are made of it, and it is made of us, whether Jackson Pollack, or a religious deity, we are united in our commonality and ordinariness, and yet our uniqueness in the context of such a vast expanse is to be cherished. We are unique in the vastness of space and can take our place in the majesty of such a remarkable environment, so too can we cherish the attributes that make us unique and capable of creativity and innovative outputs. We are selfless when we are free to be, and that freedom is gained through a trust in ourselves, and the profound abilities and attributes we all possess if awakened, or permitted to be truly connected and appreciated, firstly by ourselves to then be of value to others, both human and non-human, on and off-Earth across new worlds, and dimensions.

The screen production company, Reed Films Pty Ltd., was part of an ecosystem of other independent screen production businesses and companies in Australia.

My experiences with my company grew out of the need to discover and develop alternative modes and methods of operation for independent screen production start-ups. In this instance, Remo Media, the company's documentary production arm, served as the vehicle through which I sought alternative funding arrangements and operations for regional screen production.

Government-assisted filmmaking, whether state or Federal in Australia, leads to several restrictions with regard to sustainable screen enterprises, especially in regional areas and cities for small to medium-sized enterprises (SME) specialising in documentary or factual television programming. The location of Federal funding agencies does not favour regional producers in Australia and statistically, the majority of filmmaking takes place in the larger cities where the major agencies are situated [Office for the Arts, Department of the Prime Minister and Cabinet (DPMC) 2011; Screen Australia 2010, 2012a].

In a competitive environment, such as screen production, larger commercial centres are attractive to the institutional and informal networks of producers and filmmakers who cluster in better-serviced geographical areas (Jones et al. 2003) to seek film and digital subsidies from Federal and state government institutions supporting screen production (Office for the Arts, DPMC 2011; Screen Australia 2010).

## On Location in Adelaide, SA

My business was conducted in Adelaide, South Australia, which, in terms of screen production, is positioned regionally in an industry that is predominantly centred in other states of Australia that have greater concentrations of screen businesses and companies (Screen Australia 2012a) and the structures that support them, both from private enterprise and the public sector.

At the time of testing the business, government support of the screen production sector was undergoing significant structural changes that influenced my activities (Office for the Arts, DPMC 2011; Screen Australia 2010). Reed Films Pty Ltd. was built upon the market experience and operations of an earlier media production business known in the market as Remo Media. Reed Films Pty Ltd. was formed on 19 May 2008, subsuming Remo Media, although the latter continued as the trading name of the company. Remo Media/Reed Films, an entrepreneurial, emergent company, provided an essential structure needed in order to see what could be achieved as a film entrepreneur.

Remo Media/Reed Films was included in a quantitative survey conducted by Screen Australia, which produced data that resulted in seminal documents consulted during my efforts to appreciate the task at hand. The documents were the 2010 Review of the Australian Independent Screen Production Sector (Office for the Arts, DPMC 2011) and the Submission to the Australian Government's 2010 Review of the Independent Screen Production Sector (Screen Australia 2010).

The South Australian Film Corporation (SAFC), on behalf of the South Australian government, in partnership with the Australian Broadcasting Corporation (ABC), developed an initiative entitled the FACTory for factual entertainment (SAFC 2010). The FACTory initiative aimed to get more media production in South Australia, and resulted in a Senate inquiry [Australian Broadcasting Corporation (ABC) 2011; Harris 2011; Senate Environment and Communications References Committee (SECRC) 2011, 2012] and highlighted the issue of direct support as opposed to indirect support for the media arts, which had been raised prior to earlier reforms [Australian Film Commission (AFC) 2006, 4] to the screen production sector (Office for the Arts, DPMC 2011; Screen Australia 2010).

Although the quantitative evidence offered by national and state screen agencies responsible for the screen production sector attempts always to focus on the positive (Screen Australia 2012a), any filmmaker who operates from a regional city or regional area is in reality disadvantaged with regard to documentary production opportunities. It is important to remember, however, that the independent screen production sector in Australia is reliant upon government assistance provided by agencies whose existence is justified on the basis of statistical evidence in support of initiatives and programmes (Office for the Arts, DPMC 2011; Screen Australia 2010). For the producer of documentary programmes, the reality behind any statistics is the reason I thought I might seek new strategies for gaining support for independent producers from South Australia (and elsewhere) attempting to access funding for production. New strategies would have implications for national and international funding bodies or agencies and how direct and indirect funding affects the market and its constituents.

## The Nature of the Problem

A total of 343 hours of first-release Australian documentaries (including co-productions) were broadcast on Australian free-to-air TV in 2007, including 137 hours by the ABC and 88 hours by SBS (Special Broadcasting Service). This is the highest level in the ten-year period back to 1998 and significantly higher than the average (283 hours).

There was, however, a disjunction between public and private investors in Australian documentaries. The documentary's impact and success, and clearly quantity, did not equal the perceived quality (as far as the audience was indicating) that was implicitly required by government sector supported screen products. Through the agency of my company, it became clear that the accepted pathway of public-funded documentary production was open to an innovation, and a movement towards an approach that represented a revolutionary transition in terms of conceptual understanding of procuring funding for film projects was required.

Firstly, the initial research indicated that the selection of film topics by Australian producers, operating in the commercial market, was motivated by the necessity to attract an audience to secure income from advertising, and commercial stations regard the value of ratings success highly (Barry 2009; Stone 2007). Secondly, the producers do not pursue awards and the film festival circuit domestically or internationally as the benefit for commercial return from this activity is limited, unless a component of the production is financed from government sources. When looked at holistically, it appeared that a new perspective of the market was required when production companies planned and attempted to finance their products.

Commercial stations prefer to achieve market exposure elsewhere and do so by interacting with their audience. This leaves open the question of what the difference is between public and private broadcasters in terms of documentary production and why there is such delineation in the marketplace. What is the market for simple documentary products and programmes?

The pursuit of profit rather than policy is generally the defining motivation for the actors within the screen production sector; and knowledge to inform dealings with the sectors of broadcasting (Office for the Arts, DPMC 2011; Screen Australia 2010) is key for an independent producer to successfully transact for the production and broadcast of programmes and products. There are advantages conferred by knowledge and experience for dealing with both public (Verhoeven 2010) and private funders (Jackson and Court 2010; Sibley 2006).

Information regarding documentary production, as well as other formats, was instrumental to the direction that I took with the creation of Remo Media/Reed Films as a real-world organisation through which I could test myself in the documentary film industry. The combination of a general purpose company and a documentary specialist company was critical to searching for funding.

The public government sector was initially regarded as essential for access to seed monies and industry support. However, dependence on this form of screen production is unsustainable and flawed as a perpetuating model for production when it becomes path dependent. The 'subsidy model' of film and digital production (Verhoeven 2010, 133–154) can entrap the producer who believes in it and surrenders to its containment. Failure to look outside the path dependence of the producer's reliance on the 'subsidy model' is a result of insufficient examination of structural processes (Liebowitz and Margolis 1995a, b; Welch 2001).

Seeking to path diverge and re-route (Chandrashekar et al. 2005) is desirable because divergence and flexibility are required to avoid dependence and ultimately disempowerment (Mannix 2013; South Australian Film Corporation Strategic Plan 2012; South Australian Film Corporation Strategic Review Phase 2 2013; Screen Production Investment 2013).

The importance of this insight into funding paths was that it enabled a reflection upon a system that constantly presented statistics and evidence of an industry that seemed to be thriving, however was not. An unadulterated appraisal of the documentary programme market in Australia was therefore pursued as part of identifying new funding paths. Path dependency impacted upon the psyche, process and operations of an entity in this marketplace of 'subsidised' and 'bureaucratised' visual content delivery, and awareness of this fact was critical to the development of the new company.

In 2008, documentaries reached a peak of 445 hours in Australia, a figure that presented an apex for several years, despite substantial reforms to the screen production sector and international increases in documentary production and distribution (Rampell 2013; Screen Australia 2015a, b).

Current screen production sector funding in Australia to support projects and business development requires written applications adhering to the guidelines, policies and goals of the funding institution, often being a state or Federal government that is encouraging the development and growth of film or screen culture and its industry (Screen Australia 2012a, b, c).

A film producer may accept government funds as an interest bearing investment, which is repayable. Alternatively, the funds may be a grant, which does not require repayment (Screen Australia 2010).

The Australian Bureau of Statistics (ABS) and Screen Australia provide statistical information regarding national screen production, which in the area of documentary productions demonstrates that producers outside major commercial centres in Australia are less likely to be prolific in this genre (Screen Australia 2012a). Government financially assisted programming in documentary production (Film Australia 2006) adheres to a bureaucratic framework that may inhibit and stifle the growth of businesses, including regional areas, with long delays and complicated funding requirements (Connolly 2008; Jackson and Court 2010; Verhoeven 2010; Weir 2013).

Both in Australia (Screen Australia 2012b) and internationally (Jackson and Court 2010; Olsberg 2012), support for producers of programming for broad and narrowcast outlets (Boreham 2012) and theatrical distribution is growing. However, Screen Australia and the Australian Taxation Office (ATO) implemented the Producer Offset (2009) and Qualifying Australian Production Expenditure (QAPE) in 2008 (Calder 2011; Screen Australia 2008, 2010, 2012b) to assist the development, through fiscal sustainability, of the screen production sector in Australia.

The established pathway that my company examined during the research study was bureaucratic by nature and instituted by government policy. It was therefore inherently political (Matthews 1988), without necessarily giving consideration to economic and social objectives that would be addressed by supporting and developing screen production in Australia (Office for the Arts, DPMC 2011), New Zealand (Jackson and Court 2010) and elsewhere in the world (Olsberg 2012).

The bureaucratic model is marked by inefficiencies due to a range of inherent elements, especially in relation to the independent screen production sector and its culture of fiscal support in Australia (Mannix 2013; Sayer-Jones 2014, 62; Verhoeven 2010, 137–139), which is limited by its administrative processes. When bureaucracy is viewed in relation to government support of the sector, it can be seen as an essentially positivist (Horkheimer 1974) structure, especially when it is used in the most politically expedient way (Matthews 1988).

If the objective of government seed money, whether project-based or as an enterprise initiative, is to launch screen businesses, then this must always be a focal point of support (Office for the Arts, DPMC 2011; Screen Australia 2010). The government institution, in such circumstances, is ostensibly the mentor or parent body that is guiding the fledgling infant company or business towards independence and self-sustaining autonomy (Jackson and Court 2010).

The fiscal planning of a business venture is essential to an independent production model in the screen production sector (Office for the Arts, DPMC 2011; Screen Australia 2010). It is neither advisable nor fiscally sustainable to focus on creative work alone. The work must be, however, an essential part of a package of product and production that provides return-on-investment (ROI) and can launch successful businesses and producers of film and digital works (Jackson and Court 2010, 17).

It should be noted that debate regarding artistic endeavour in relation to commercial consideration has continued for decades among government funding agencies and the screen production sector, as well as in the broader community (Verhoeven 2010, 139–142).

At the beginning of the journey with my company, information regarding documentary production, as well as other formats, was instrumental to the direction that the research took and informed the creation of what would later be the very important development of a manifesto or creed (a written statement that describes the policies, goals and opinions of a person or group) which became integral to the activities of the company, and was adhered to by Remo Media/Reed Films.

The company of which I was the secretary, co-director and co-principal acted independently without considering other entities or companies in the marketplace, except for the transformative examples of loosely termed 'creative entrepreneurs', trends or government programmes. The manifesto for Remo Media/Reed Films focused on learning by planning, doing and reflecting, and the possibility of acquiring radical knowledge.

The *parabolic scramble* illustrates the movement of the entrepreneur and entrepreneurial enterprise through an industry-agnostic ecosystem towards a multitude of ecosystems, termed the entrepreneurial multiverse. This is further developed and enhanced using the additional qualities provided by augmented, to CMR technological applications.

## The Unfolding Journey

My unfolding journey as an entrepreneur in media incorporating film, screen, audio, digital, expanded and contracted, twisted and turned as the experience delivered unexpected findings. The shifts of focus, the planning, acting, observing and reflecting to then plan, act, observe and reflect again generated an extremely flexible framework to work within (Galilei 1914), very similar to my experience as a researcher.

I used my emergent company in tandem with action research to conduct an intimate examination of an industry that is cloaked in complex layers of bureaucracy and political legacy (Verhoeven 2010).

Faced with a problem, the action researcher goes through a series of phases (plan, act, observe, reflect) referred to as the action research cycle to systematically tackle the problem (Dick 1997).

*Action learning is perhaps best understood as a working philosophy rather than a set of techniques or standard practices. A distinction can be made between action learning as a specific method and its wider influence as an 'ethos' or general way of thinking. (Pedler and Burgoyne* 2015, *180)*

In practice, things rarely go according to plan first time round, and the plan is improved in light of experience and feedback. One cycle of planning, acting, observing and reflecting, therefore usually leads to another, in which you incorporate improvements suggested by the initial cycle. Projects often do not fit neatly into a cycle of planning, action, observation and reflection. It is perfectly legitimate to follow a somewhat disjointed process if circumstances dictate (see Fig. 2.3).

As has been seen with quantum mechanics and its theory, there is a basis for an understanding and appreciation of 'uncertainty' which is at the

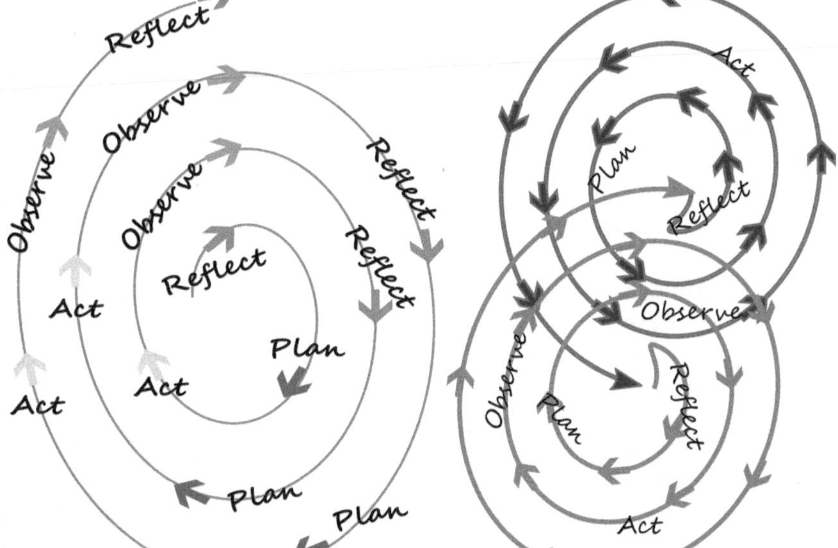


**Fig. 2.3** The action research cycle (or spiral/s) is also typical of the experience of action learning. Action learning is, however, much more associated with groups of learners or a programme of action learning within an organisation. (Prepared by Author and based on Dick 1997)

core of the universe and as Albert Einstein would ultimately acknowledge is in our consciousness as human beings (Hawking 1988; Penrose 2011). Elements of 'uncertainty' became evident in the volatility that began to be encountered through the experiences of Remo Media/Reed Films.

My emergent company consistently adjusted its approach as I increased in knowledge, understanding and experience, and a phenomenon emerged that I named the *parabolic scramble* which fed into the Barnes Dance Principle (Jaffe 2012; James 1997, 182–206; Rosen 1985; von Bertalanffy 1968).

*Parabolic Scramble and the Barnes Dance Principle* The *parabolic scramble* was conceived when my learning with Remo Media/Reed Films was just beginning, and proved to be a useful metaphor for my experience. The concept of the *parabolic scramble* depicts my experience of action research as highly volatile and fluid. The term as noted earlier was conceived when I was crossing a major intersection at a pedestrian 'scramble crossing' (Fig. 2.4). Importantly while crossing on a number of occasions, I could not proceed in a straight line because of the many other pedestrians, even cyclists, and people with bags, stacked boxes on trolleys and prams whose movement had to be observed and avoided. It is the obstacle that so often provides the opportunity for our insight as we contemplate its existence, and seek an alternative pathway. The situation was, indeed, a 'scramble' that, when analysed, tended to ultimately take the form of a series of parabolas (Figs. 2.4, 2.5 and 2.6) and, virtually, 'dance' steps.

While I could skirt the clot of people occupying the greatest area of the scramble in a parabolic fashion, there could still be approaches and retreats, stops and turns in order to move towards my goal. The situation was very dynamic. This put me in mind of an alternate name applied to these types of crossing–Barnes Dance–associated with the traffic engineer, Henry Barnes (1906–1968), who further developed the concept in the USA.

The concept of a dance amidst a parabolic movement soon became integrated into events as the Barnes Dance Principle and became a bridge between action research as depicted in the literature and the way the emergent company experienced action research as the market was interpreted and interaction with the market was understood, whether in the context of private enterprise or the public sector. The *parabolic scramble* cum dance became a versatile way of interpreting and describing a range of interactions for the emergent company, inspired by a fortuitous

**Fig. 2.4** Image of a scramble crossing, X-crossing or Barnes Dance. (Photograph by Author)

interaction with a scramble crossing in the centre of the city of Adelaide at an early stage. However, this was at an earlier juncture and would be an iterative development on the progression towards a more complex understanding, and application of the *parabolic scramble.*

I realised that I did not have to follow the guidelines for the scramble crossing when I became aware that I could skirt the variables within its boundaries represented by pedestrians within the parameters of its formalised structure (Barnes 1965, 103–117). The outcome was not, nor could it be, predetermined; thus, I could see flexibility as the key to successful research and entrepreneurship. The *planning, acting, observing* and *reflecting* happened more rapidly than I expected. The phenomenon was not only actual but had a psychological effect on the pursuit of my goal.

**Fig. 2.5** Time-lapse delay of pedestrians using a scramble crossing (Barnes Dance). Following the time-lapse movement of the actor in the rounded yellow rectangle, we can see how a parabola can emerge as he, she, they selects an alternate route when encountering the person in orange. The actor in the blue rectangle 'dances' among the people he, she, they passes. The Barnes Dance Principle says that entrepreneurs will be faced with obstacles when attempting to reach their goals (e.g. funding), just as pedestrians face obstructions in a scramble crossing. They must react flexibly in order to avoid being blocked. They must be willing to change direction without losing sight of their goals when faced with challenges. (Prepared by Author from a time-lapse photograph by Sam Javanrouh of a scramble crossing at Toronto, Canada sourced from:- http://wvs.topleftpixel.com/photos/2008/08/yongedundas_scramble_milestones_max_01.jpg)

## Experiencing the *Parabolic Scramble*: The Filmmaker as Entrepreneur

I am a filmmaker specialising in documentary, and later factual entertainment, an entrepreneur and a researcher. The *parabolic scramble* was the name I gave to the action learning/research framework through which I interpreted the actions of the emergent company while we sought to develop IP and support for its future sustainability.

Michael Peters and Tina Besley (2008) cite an important point, pertinent to the development of the *parabolic scramble* framework when discussing a notion of creativity as put forward by John Howkins, the

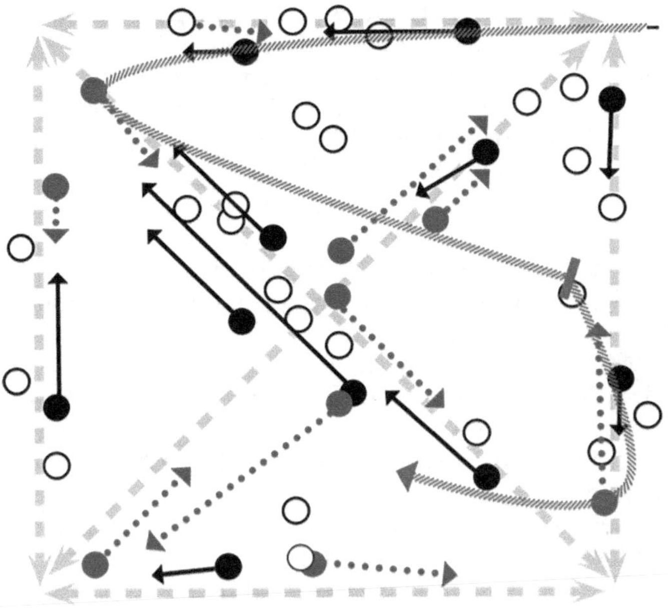

**Fig. 2.6** The *parabolic scramble* framework as part of the Barnes Dance Principle is illustrated here by the combination of circles and lines, including the wide, mauve dashed line in the shape of a parabola. The parabolic shape emerges when an individual agent decides to move differently from everyone else. Since the concept is temporal as well as physical, changes in direction or unusual movements must be compensated for in the temporal plane. (Concept and preparation by Author).

then-deputy chairman of the British Screen Advisory Council and a Governor of the London Film School. Howkins (2001) suggests that

> *Everyone can be creative as it ... is personal and subjective...innovation is group led, ... and objective. Creativity can lead to innovation. Innovation seldom leads to creativity. (88)*

This observation is analogous to experiencing the *parabolic scramble* while developing a media product. I used the concept of the *parabolic scramble* to shine a lens on a range of issues facing the filmmaker as an entrepreneur and to provide the means of interpreting diverse scenarios, theoretically and philosophically, as well as in practical applications of mode and method, for Remo Media/Reed Films (James 1997, 182–206; Rosen 1985; von Bertalanffy 1968). Once the scramble had been recognised, it was realised that it was a means of conducting research with Remo Media/Reed Films to determine how funding could be secured (David 1986, 1997, 1999, 2000; Puffert 2000, 2002, 2004) and path dependent lock-in avoided (Liebowitz and Margolis 1995a, b). Lessons learned would inform the future progression of Remo Media/Reed Films, perhaps serving as a predictive device for future planning and strategy.

Ultimately, the emergent company (operating in the initial stages as Remo Media by retaining the former business name until the establishment of Reed Films Pty Ltd in the marketplace) adopted the concept of the *parabolic scramble*, absorbing it as part of its deoxyribonucleic acid (DNA). The capacity to adjust to circumstances when moving from point A to point B meant that Remo Media/Reed Films had in its repertoire a device that an entrepreneur could use broadly across its planning and funding stages. The concept proved to be of immense commercial and practical value and continues to hold its currency during recent activities (Barney 2001; Penrose and Pitelis 2009) of Remo Media/Reed Films as the company gained traction in the market.

Illustrated by the scramble crossing, the *parabolic scramble* is an aspect of the intersection of the public and private sectors as funding sources (Barnes 1965, 103–117; Verhoeven 2010; Weir 2013). Remo Media/Reed Films had to navigate the public and private sectors in order to fund its activities. Although the company entered the market on a predetermined line, 'scrambling' would clearly be required to make the most of funding alternatives in the marketplace. In this way, the framework enabled the company to deal with action in real time with an anticipatory element that is nimble due to the framework's inherently flexible space.

Complex negotiations were required on the part of Remo Media/Reed Films when dealing with the market alternatives to current market conventions. The emergent company found a range of funding possibilities, combined with production uncertainties, possible for a regionally sited screen production company and the rapidity with which negotiations and choices must be made and the rapidity of the consequences of those choices.

Government seed money is often integral to the success of a media entrepreneur in Australia specialising in documentary screen production. Remo Media's broadcast documentary *Missing: Presumed Dead* (2012), for example, was marred by long development periods and delays due to a funding model that was dependent upon government-assisted production pathways. Valuable time and opportunity can be lost due to the arbitrary nature of decisions made by persons following an agenda that is bureaucratic (Verhoeven 2010, 137–141) or limited by personal worldview, experience or preference (Matthews 1988, 13–14). The gatekeeper may be one or two persons or several and the process is often not transparent (Jackson and Court 2010, 7–17; SAFC 2012, 17; Thom 2007, 16), although increasingly attempts to empower screen producers are occurring (Screen Australia 2012b, 2013a; Screen Australia Strategic Plan 2012–2015, 2012).

The gatekeepers may be other filmmakers, although they may not necessarily be the most appropriate person to sit in judgement of a potential rival filmmaker's project or pitch (Swift 2009, 8 and 38). There are exceptions to the rule. However, the very nature of such a dynamic represents a conflict of interest of an obvious and potentially counter-productive nature (Crook 2012; *Screen Australia Conflict of Interest Policy* 2010; Screen Australia 2010; *South Australian Film Corporation Act* 1972 2011; Thom 2007, 16).

Probity in government institutions is not the central issue for the film and digital producer (Jackson and Court 2010), although it has been an ongoing issue that has been addressed previously (Thom 2007). The gatekeepers are so numerous in multi-level financed projects that both private and public funding become complicated by process and a disjunction between the institutional outlook and the actual experience of conducting business in the free marketplace (Screen Hub 2013; Verhoeven 2010, 137–141; Weir 2013).

Data to inform the activities, reflections and plans of the emergent company were gathered from a range of sources, including published materials specific to independent screen production, especially the 2010 Review of the Australian Independent Screen Production Sector (2011) and the Submission to the Australian Government's 2010 Review of the Independent Screen Production Sector (Screen Australia 2010) to which Remo Media/Reed Films had contributed through participating in a survey. While attempting to secure support for Remo Media/Reed Films' delivery of documentaries to free-to-air and subscription television, I kept a journal to record events, objectives and outcomes related to every plan, activity and result, with the ultimate goal of providing an example of a screen production company with a tested and redefined pathway towards financial autonomy.

In documenting the process of finding funding for the emergent business and studying other relevant sources, I was able to operate in real time and became conscious of path dependency (David 1986, 1997, 1999, 2000; Puffert 2000, 2001, 2002, 2004, 2009) in relation to the support of independent screen production in Australia that had become heavily invested economically and politically systemically in the financial subsidy of that sector. The ingrained culture was so dependent upon subsidy and to such an extent that path dependency had to be understood in order for Remo Media/Reed Films to comprehend the dynamic of screen production, which I found was difficult to review unless path dependency was applied as a filter to the existing financing structure.

Indeed, I became conscious of the path dependency influencing my own approach to screen production financing, as subsidy had become an accepted culture within a screen production industry relying upon government largesse for its survival. To this end, the framework of the *parabolic scramble* helped me understand that I would need to change things by degrees to realise their potential; this was the value of an experiment in real-time markets.

## Remo Media/Reed Films

The research study was grounded in qualitative action research with a particular emphasis on participation (Shank 2006) by establishing a real-world company and adopting a constructivist (Berger and Luckmann 1967) position.

*A Company Was Created* On 19 May 2008 Remo Media was subsumed by Reed Films Pty Ltd., which retained Remo Media as a trading name with the intention that it would become the documentary (Film Australia 2006; *Screen Australia Act 2008* 2013) specialist for Reed Films. Together the two entities continued, formed as a film (screen) company for the purposes of the study. It has been referred to as Remo Media/Reed Films. Remo Media/Reed Films Produced Documentaries A *documentary* is the '… creative treatment of reality, other than as news, current affairs, sports coverage, magazine, infotainment or light entertainment …' (Australian Broadcasting Authority 2004, 3). As modified for the *Tax and Superannuation Laws Amendment Bill* 2013, a documentary is further defined as, *having regard to the extent and purpose of any contrived situation featured in the [documentary] and ... the extent to which the [documentary] explores an idea or a theme; and ... the extent to which the [documentary] has an overall narrative structure and any other relevant matters. (House of Representatives* 2013, *10)*

There were crucially important steps that the participatory company needed to embark upon in order to transform its position in the South Australian screen market which was deemed by it as untenable.

The first stage was to remove the participatory company from the local screen sector in order to reflect upon practice and potential inhibitors and also learn insights from other industries. As it transpired, this was a core developmental position to adopt for the participatory company and although it was difficult in the initial stages this was an essential starting point.

The next stage was to reconstitute the participatory company in a constructivist mode to re-strategise and re-engage with existent products, and this led to negotiations with national broadcasters, which were successfully achieved using the documentary *Missing: Presumed Dead* as the test case documentary programme that essentially launched Remo Media/Reed Films and has provided the basis upon which engagement with the national and international screen markets was built. There were to be many transformative events for the company. Further crucial transformations would include the identification of path dependency.

*Straight-Talk* Remo Media, prior to the establishment of Reed Films Pty Ltd., had as its first assignment a documentary about the criminal justice system of the South Australian city of Adelaide and its environs, including Northfield Women's Prison, Yatala Labour Prison and Mobilong Prison with serving detainees, on internal and external programmes providing the production of visually delivered required components. Remo Media was the only film business, at that time, to record visual and audio material at Yatala Labour Prison's high-security G-Division. The subsequent documentary, *Straight-talk,* has since been viewed throughout South Australia and at international conventions on crime prevention. The documentary was funded privately within the framework of the criminal justice and correctional systems.

The Criminal Justice and Correctional departments operated formally, as would be expected of a government bureaucracy, and also presented challenges due to the ever-changing political landscape of government administration and policy. All members of the programme, from serving detainees to the Chief Executive Officer (CEO) and Parliamentary Ministers, were supportive and contributory to the processes and procedural requirements of Remo Media.

Nevertheless, subsequent involvement with government bureaucracy and film production would never be straightforward. The experience of dealing with and managing relationships through government bureaucracy and its agents can be seen as a part of an expected reflective learning process.

As part of reviewing the funding experience, Remo Media/Reed Films sought to determine the nature and the value of its enterprise (Drucker 2004, 231–234) and position the company commercially. A desire to circumvent bureaucracy led to the pursuit of alternative pathways in which Remo Media/Reed Films developed IP in ways that supported its independence in the marketplace; and avoided complicated and often ineffective avenues of financing and production support offered by government screen agencies. These attempts illustrated the nascent experiences that would later inform the *parabolic scramble* and its action. All elements of the search for viability and a lengthy discourse with bureaucracy in its many forms were incorporated as an adjunct to the creative work necessary to supply screen products to the market.

The Department of Correctional Services eventually withdrew permission for the detainees from the prison system to participate directly in the production of *Straight-talk* because they felt that their agreement with specific screen content providers and media outlets, prior to Remo Media's involvement, had portrayed the criminal justice system inaccurately.

This change in plans led Remo Media to enlarge its creative parameters and explore new ways to tell their story, which enhanced the product. This flexibility and ability to shift ground is an example of the *parabolic scramble* framework. Out of perceived chaos (Burns 2002, 42–44; Field and Golubitsky 1992; Gleick 1987; Levy 1994, 167–178) grew new modes of creation at all levels of endeavour. The reality was that the required changes marked the development of the project and were key to its success among serving detainees in representing their specific and individual stories of incarceration and its life impact.

The *parabolic scramble*, on reflection, demonstrated clearly the way in which path dependency (David 1986, 1997, 1999, 2000; Puffert 2000, 2001, 2002, 2004, 2009) was evident in many forms in relation to the emergent company's engagement with the market and its actors, because it offered a different pathway through a different approach. This *parabolic scramble* by its very configuration enabled a questioning of the norm and allowed its reinterpretation to find an alternative pathway. And, to my mind, while it mimicked the action learning/research cycle, the scramble more accurately reflected my actual lived experience because of the inherent dynamism and irregularity it represented.

## Missing: Presumed Dead

*Missing: Presumed Dead* was a documentary for television that has been screened repeatedly since 2008 in Australia, on The History Channel (later changed to History), as seen on Foxtel.

The project was financially assisted with development investment from the South Australian Film Corporation (SAFC), the Australian Film Commission (AFC), now known as Screen Australia and ABC and was used as a test case for the research investigation as it provided the engagement necessary with broadcasters, both in the public and private markets for documentary programming. In much the same way as the documentaries produced in the Criminal Justice System of South Australia (*Nine Women of Northfield: Tales from within* and *Straight-talk*) had been foundationally important to Remo Media's early commercial experience so too *Missing: Presumed Dead* would provide another point of transformative benefit for the developing participatory company.

*Missing: Presumed Dead* was, therefore, the pathfinder (Mann 2001; Morrell and Capparell 2003; Shackleton 1995, 4; Soanes and Stevenson 2004, 1049) enterprise for a slate of projects ready for development when Remo Media/Reed Films was organised. The production was a model of a documentary that found an audience and was well received, but which did not offer a sustainable fiscal model of screen creation for the producer of film and digital works to use in the future. This observation was consistent with a range of other works and companies, and I became interested in determining the tipping point or transformational moment (Cranton 1994, 1996; Mezirow 1991, 1995, 1996, 2000, 3–31) of sustainability, and ultimately a viable method of financing for film and digital production.

The history of the financing for *Missing: Presumed Dead* produced a range of benefits. Although the project was ultimately realised with a reduced budget, and not the original pathway of financing, the outcome was an independently produced documentary with greater editorial input from the originator because the limitations forced more creativity, although at the expense of a longer development process.

When the research began, I developed a 12-month plan to launch Remo Media/Reed Films. A three-year projection was prepared with the goal of securing cash flow and becoming self-sufficient to ultimately achieve growth. Niche screen business portals for distribution to the broadest market were sought to become part of the strategic planning and procedures undertaken as the business was developed.

Remo Media as part of Reed Films had (and continues to have though is transitioning to Refutured to incorporate CMR developments and applications) a range of market developed projects that have been presented to screen markets, in both public and commercial contexts, that represent a substantial investment by the participatory company in IP for commercial endeavours and market explorations. The unknown element has always been the distribution of these works, by a variety of systems to consumers, which might not at the time of undertaking the research exist (James 1997, 182–206; Rosen 1985; von Bertalanffy 1968).

I was aware that systems of delivery might become redundant, or incorporated into technological advances that rendered the propositions and investigations outmoded, and lacking currency in marketplace dialogue (Frith 2012; Mason 2008). The action research I had experienced had taught me to keep pushing for answers to complex questions, such as those posed by a film and digital company seeking commercial sustainability and growth, regarding the global marketplace especially in the context of a company that has regional environs as an entry point.

The ability to reflect and evaluate the public sector and private enterprise in relation to entrepreneurial, and intrapreneurial endeavour, has emerged as an area that requires further examination by those involved in the arts (Zolin and Kropp 2008, 2009, 2010), and could provide remarkable benefits for the screen production sector in Australia and overseas.

## Bibliography

Australian Broadcasting Authority. 2004. *Documentary Guidelines: Interpretation of 'Documentary' for the Australian Content Standard.* Commonwealth of Australia, Sydney.

Australian Film Commission. 2006. Submission to the Department of Communications Information Technology and the Arts: Review of Australian Government Funding Support. Canberra: Australian Government Australian Film Commission.

Australian Taxation Office. 2009. *Producer Offset-Timing of Claims-Liquidation Option.* Australian Government Australian Taxation Office.

Barnes HA. 1965. *The Man with the Red and Green Eyes: The Autobiography of Henry A. Barnes, Traffic Commissioner, New York City.* New York: E P Dutton & Co.

Barney J. 2001. "Is the Resource-based 'View' a Useful Perspective for Strategic Management Research? Yes." *Academy of Management Review* 26, no. 1: 41–56.

Barry P. 2009. *Who Wants to be a Billionaire? The James Packer Story.* Sydney: Allen & Unwin.

Berger PL, Luckmann T. 1967. *The Social Construction of Reality.* London: Allen Lane The Penguin Press.

Boreham, G. 2012. *Convergence Review: Final Report.* Department of Broadband, Communications and the Digital Economy (Australia), Australia Government. https://apo.org.au/node/29219

Burns J. 2002. "Chaos Theory and Leadership studies: Exploring Uncharted Seas." *Journal of Leadership and Organisation Studies* 9, no. 2: 42–56.

Calder T. 2011. *Screen Australia Welcomes Funding Increase and Producer Offset Reform.* Screen Australia, 10 May.

Chandrashekar J, Duan Z, Klansky J, Zhang Z. 2005. "Limiting Path Exploration in BGP." 24th Annual Joint Conference of the IEEE Computer and Communications Societies. *Proceedings of the IEEE INFOCOM* 4: 2337–2348, Miami, 13–17 March.

Connolly R. 2008. *Embracing Innovation: A New Methodology for Feature Film Production in Australia.* AFTRS Centre for Screen Business. Canberra: Australian Government Australian Government Australian Film Television and Radio School.

Cooper B, Vlaskovits, P. 2016. *The Lean Entrepreneur: How Visionaries Create Products, Innovate with New Ventures, and Disrupt Markets.* New York: Wiley & Sons.

Cranton P. 1994. *Understanding and Promoting Transformative Learning: A Guide for Educators of Adults.* San Francisco: Jossey-Bass Publishers.

Cranton P. 1996. *Professional Development as Transformative Learning: New Perspectives for Teachers of Adults.* San Francisco: Jossey-Bass Publishers.

Crook A. 2012. "Screen Australia Says No Conflict Over Film Funding." *Crikey*. http://www.crikey.com.au/2012/03/27/screen-australia-says-no-rats-in-our-ranks-over-film-funding/

David P. 1986. "Understanding the Economics of QWERTY: The Necessity of History." In W Parker (ed). *Economic History and the Modern Economist*. Oxford: Blackwell: 30–49.

David P. 1997. "Path Dependence and the Quest for Historical Economics: One More Chorus of the Ballad of QWERTY." University of Oxford Discussion Papers in Economic and Social History, no. 20. http://www.nuff.ox.ac.uk/economics/history/paper20/david3.pdf.

David P. 1999. "At Last, A Remedy for Chronic QWERTY-Skepticism!" Working Paper. All Souls College, Oxford University. https://econpapers.repec.org/paper/wopstanec/99025.htm

David P. 2000. *Path Dependence, its Critics and the Quest for Historical Economics*. All Souls College. Oxford: Oxford University.

DeadlineDetroit. 2019. *Mike Duggan Transition Team Quotes Winston Churchill, Gets Quote Wrong*. https://www.deadlinedetroit.com/articles/7285/mike_duggan_transition_team_quotes_winston_churchill_gets_quote_wrong

Dick B. 1997. "Action Learning and Action Research." *Resource Papers in Action Research*. http://www.aral.com.au/resources/actlearn.html.

Drucker PF. 2004. *Innovation and Entrepreneurship*. Oxford: Butterworth-Heinemann.

Field M, Golubitsky M. 1992. *Symmetry in Chaos: A Search for Pattern in Mathematics, Art and Nature*. Oxford: Oxford University Press.

Film Australia. 2006. *Review of Australian Government Film Funding Support Submission*. Government of Australia. https://apo.org.au/sites/default/files/resource-files/2007-06/apo-nid15305.pdf.

Frith D. 2012. "Joining the Stream of IPTV Promises to Cut Cable and Costs." *The Australian*.

Galilei G. 1914. *Dialogues Concerning Two New Sciences*. Trans H Crew, A De Salvio and A Favaro (intro). New York: The Macmillan Company. https://oll.libertyfund.org/title/galilei-dialogues-concerning-two-new-sciences.

Glaser BG, Strauss AL. 1967. *The Discovery of Grounded Theory: Strategies for Qualitative Research*. Chicago: Aldine Publishing Company.

Gleick J. 1987. *Chaos-Making a New Science*. Middlesex: Penguin Books.

Harris R. 2011. *Question on Notice-enquiry Regarding ABC Programming: FACTory Initiatives Information*. Canberra: Department of the Senate. https://apo.org.au/sites/default/files/resource-files/2011-10/apo-nid26848.pdf

Hawking S. 1988. *A Brief History of Time*. New York: Bantam Dell Publishing Group.

Horkheimer M. 1974. *Eclipse of Reason*. New York: Seabury Press.

House of Representatives. 2013. *Tax and Superannuation Laws Amendment (2013 Measures no. 2) Bill 2013*. Parliament of the Commonwealth of Australia. https://www.aph.gov.au/Parliamentary_Business/Bills_Legislation/Bills_Search_Results/Result?bId=r5013.

Howkins J. 2001. *The Creative Economy: How People Make Money from Ideas*. London: Allen Lane.

Jackson, P, Court, D. 2010. "Review of the New Zealand Film Commission." A Report to the Hon Chris Finlayson, MP, Minister for the Arts, Culture & Heritage. Wellington.

Jaffe E. 2012. "A Brief History of the Barnes Dance." *The Atlantic Cities*. 18 December. http://www.theatlanticcities.com/commute/2012/12/brief-history-barnes-dance/4189/

James J. 1997. *Thinking in the Future Tense*. New York: Touchstone.

Jones D, Barlow J, Finlay S, Savage H. 2003. *NZfilm: A Case Study of the New Zealand Film Industry*. Wellington: Competitive Advantage New Zealand.

Levy D. 1994. "Chaos Theory and Strategy: Theory, Application, and Managerial Implications." *Strategic Management Journal* 15, no. 2: 167–178.

Liebowitz S, Margolis S. 1995a. Path Dependence, Lock-in, and History. *Journal of Law, Economics, and Organization* 11, no. 1: 205–226.

Liebowitz S, Margolis S. 1995b. "Policy and Path Dependence: From QWERTY to *Windows* 95." *Regulation: The Cato Review of Business & Government* 18, no. 3: 33–41.

List D. 2002. *Know Your Audience: A Practical Guide to Media Research*. 3rd ed. Wellington: Original Books.

List D. 2005. "Social Network Mapping: The Development of a Methodology for Social Enquiry." PhD Thesis. The University of South Australia, Adelaide.

Lorenz EN. 1972. "Predictability: Does the Flap of a Butterfly's Wings in Brazil Set off a Tornado in Texas?" American Association for the Advancement of Science, 139th Meeting. Sheraton Park Hotel, 29 December. http://eaps4.mit.edu/research/Lorenz/Butterfly_1972.pdf.

Mandelbrot B. 1977. *Fractals: Form. Chance and Dimension*. New York: W H Freeman and Company.

Mandelbrot B. 1982. *The Fractal Geometry of Nature*. New York: W H Freeman and Company.

Mann S. 2001. "Shackleton's Way: Leadership Lessons from the Great Antarctic Explorer." *Leadership & Organization Development Journal* 22, no. 6: 301–303.

Mannix L. 2013. "Film Corp Has Less Money, But More 'Mouths To Feed'." *Indaily*. 30 January.

Mason M. 2008. *The Pirate's Dilemma: How Youth Culture is Reinventing Capitalism*. New York: Free Press.

Matthews C. 1988. *Hardball: How Politics is Played Told by One Who Knows The Game*. New York: Harper Perennial.

Mezirow J. 1991. *Transformative Dimensions of Adult Learning*. San Francisco: Jossey-Bass Publishers.

Mezirow J. 1995. "Transformative Theory of Adult Learning." In M Welton (ed). *In Defense of the Lifeworld*. Albany: State University of New York Press: 39–70.

Mezirow J. 1996. "Contemporary Paradigms of Learning." *Adult Education Quarterly* 46, no. 3: 158–172.

Mezirow J. 2000. *Learning as Transformation: Critical Perspectives on a Theory in Progress*. San Francisco: Jossey-Bass Publishers.

Morrell M, Capparell S. 2003. *Shackleton's Way: Leadership Lessons from the Great Antarctic Explorer*. London: Nicholas Brealey Publishing Limited.

Nash J. 1950a. "Non-cooperative Games." PhD Thesis. Princeton: Princeton University. https://rbsc.princeton.edu/sites/default/files/Non-Cooperative_Games_Nash.pdf.

Nash J. 1950b. "Equilibrium Points in N-Person Games." *Proceedings of the National Academy of Sciences* 36, no. 1: 48–49.

Nash J. 1951. "Non-cooperative Games." *The Annals of Mathematics* 54, no. 2: 286–295.

Office for the Arts. 2011, 2010. *Review of the Australian Independent Screen Production Sector*. Canberra: Government of Australia Department of Prime Minister and Cabinet.

Olsberg J. 2012. *Building Sustainable Film Businesses: The Challenge for Industry and Government*. https://www.filminstitutet.se/globalassets/2.-fa-kunskap-om-film/analys-och-statistik/publications/other-publications/building-sustainable-film-businesses%2D%2D-the-challenges-for-industry.pdf.

Pedler M, Burgoyne J. 2015. "Action Learning." In H Bradbury (ed). *The Sage Handbook of Action Research*. London: SAGE Publications: 179–187.

Penrose E, Pitelis C. 2009. *The Theory of the Growth of the Firm*. Oxford: Oxford University Press.

Penrose R. 2011. Uncertainty in Quantum Mechanics: Faith or Fantasy? *Philosophical Transactions: Mathematical, Physical and Engineering Sciences* 369, no. 1956: 4864–4890.

Peters MA, Besley TAC. 2008. "Academic Entrepreneurship and the Creative Economy." *Thesis Eleven* 94, no. 1: 88–105.

Puffert D. 2000. "The Standardization of Track Gauge on North American Railways, 1830–1890." *Journal of Economic History* 60, no. 4: 933–960.

Puffert D. 2001. *Path Dependence in Spatial Networks: The Standardization of Railway Track Gauge*. Department of Economics. https://www.sciencedirect.com/science/article/abs/pii/S0014498302907862.

Puffert D. 2002. "Path Dependence in Spatial Networks: The Standardization of Railway Track Gauge." *Explorations in Economic History* 39, no. 3: 282–314.

Puffert D. 2004. "Path Dependence, Network Form, and Technological Change." In W Sundstrom, T Guinnane, and W Whatley (eds). *History Matters: Essays on*

*Economic Growth, Technology, and Demographic Change*. Stanford: Stanford University Pres.

Puffert D. 2009. *Tracks Across Continents, Paths Through History: The Economic Dynamics of Standardization in Railway Gauge*. Chicago: The University of Chicago Press.

Rampell C. 2013. "Hollywood's Biggest Bang for its Buck." *The New York Times*. Business Day. *Economix*. 9 August.

Reason P Bradbury, H. 2008. *The Sage Handbook of Action Research: Participatory Inquiry and Practice*. London: Sage Publications.

Revans R. 1980. *Action Learning: New Techniques for Management*. London: Blond & Briggs.

Revans R. 1983. "What is Action Learning?" *Journal of Management Development* 1, no. 3: 64–75.

Ries E. 2011. *The Lean Startup: How Today's Entrepreneurs Use Continuous Innovation to Create Radically Successful Businesses*. New York: Random House.

Rosen R. 1985. *Anticipatory Systems: Philosophical, Mathematical, and Methodological Foundations*. New York: Pergamon Press.

Sarasvathy SD, Venkataraman S. 2011. "Entrepreneurship as Method: Open Questions for an Entrepreneurial Future." *Entrepreneurship Theory and Practice* 35, no. 1: 113–135.

Sayer-Jones, L. 2014. *Media Law for Non-Lawyers*. Australian second edition, Double Bay: Prêt à Porter Publications.

Screen Australia Act. 2008, 2013. *Australian Government Com Law*, no. 12 2008. http://www.comlaw.gov.au/Details/C2008A00012

Screen Australia Conflict of Interest Policy. 2010. *Human Resources Policy and Guidelines*. Australian Government Screen Australia.

*Screen Australia Strategic Plan*. 2012-2015, 2012. Australian Government Screen Australia.

Screen Australia. 2008. *Australian Screen Production Incentive: Producer Offset Guidelines*. Australian Government Screen Australia.

Screen Australia. 2010. Submission to the Australian Government's 2010 Review of the Independent Screen Production Sector. Australian Government Screen Australia.

Screen Australia. 2012a. *Documentary: Number and Hours of Australian Documentaries (Not Including Broadcaster-produced Titles) by Location of Production Company, 1997 /98-2011/12*. Australian Government Screen Australia.

Screen Australia. 2012b. *Getting Down to Business: The Producer Offset Five Years On*. Australian Government Screen Australia.

Screen Australia. 2012c. *Offset Loans and Cashflow Providers*. Australian Government Screen Australia.

Screen Australia. 2013a. *Producer Offset.* Australian Government Screen Australia. http://www.screenaustralia.gov.au/producer_offset/.

Screen Australia. 2015a. *Hours of Australian Documentaries (Not Including Broadcaster-produced Titles) by Location of Production Company, 1997/98–2013/14.* Australian Government Screen Australia. https://www.screenaustralia.gov.au/fact-finders/production-trends/documentary-production/activity-summary

Screen Australia. 2015b. *Hours of First-Release Australian Documentaries Broadcast on Free-to-Air TV, 1998–2014,* Australian Government Screen Australia. http://www.screenaustralia.gov.au/research/statistics/releasesdocumentariestv.aspx.

Screen Hub. 2013. *Documentary Stoush (3): Crusaders Storm Email Barricades.* Screen Hub Industry News.

Screen Production Investment. 2013. South Australian Film Corporation. South Australia Government, Adelaide.

Senate Environment and Communications References Committee (SECRC). 2011, 2012. ABC responses to Questions on Notice: Inquiry Into Recent ABC Programming Decisions, 2011, Department of the Senate, Canberra, viewed 16 April 2022. https://www.aph.gov.au/Parliamentary_Business/Committees/Senate/Environment_and_Communications/Completed%20inquiries/2010-13/abc/report/~/media/wopapub/senate/committee/ec_ctte/completed_inquiries/2010-13/abc/report/report.ashx

Shackleton V. 1995. *Business Leadership.* London: Thomson Learning.

Shank GD. 2006. *Qualitative Research: A Personal Skills Approach.* 2nd ed. New Jersey: Pearson Merrill Prentice Hall.

Sibley B. 2006. *Peter Jackson: A Film-Maker's Journey.* Sydney: Harper Collins Publishers.

Soanes C, Stevenson A. 2004. *Concise Oxford English Dictionary.* Oxford: Oxford University Press.

*South Australian Film Corporation Act 1972.* Adelaide: South Australian Government. https://www.legislation.sa.gov.au/LZ/C/A/SOUTH%20AUSTRALIAN%20FILM%20CORPORATION%20ACT%201972.aspx.

South Australian Film Corporation. *South Australian Film Corporation Program Guideline: Special Initiatives The FACTory for Factual Entertainment. 2010.* Adelaide: South Australian Government.

South Australian Film Corporation. South Australian Film Corporation Strategic Review Issues Paper *2012.* Adelaide: South Australian Government.

South Australian Film Corporation. *South Australian Film Corporation Strategic Review Phase 2 2013.* Adelaide: South Australian Government.

South Australian Film Corporation. 2012. "Nick McMahon Breakthrough Producer Award." Media Release. South Australian Film Corporation, Adelaide, 15 November.

Stone G. 2007. *Who Killed Channel 9? The Death of Kerry Packer's Mighty Dream Machine*. Sydney: Pan Macmillan.

Submission to the Australian Government's 2010 Review of the Independent Screen Production Sector, 2010. Australian Government Screen Australia.

Swift B. 2009. No Conflict, No Interest. *Inside Film*. July: 8 & 38.

Thom V. 2007. Australian Film Commission: *Investigation into the Assessment of Film Funding Applications*. Commonwealth Ombudsman. Report no. 2. http://www.ombudsman.gov.au/__data/assets/pdf_file/0025/26296/investigation_2007_02.pdf

Verhoeven D. 2010. Film, video, DVD and Online Delivery. In S Cunningham & G Turner (eds). *The Media & Communications in Australia*. 3rd edn. Crows Nest: Allen & Unwin: 133–154.

von Bertalanffy L. 1968. *General System Theory: Foundations, Development, Applications*. New York: George Braziller.

Weir D. 2013. *How Sustainable is the Australian Content Production Industry?* Keynote address presented at the Australian International Documentary Conference. Adelaide, 25–28 February.

Welch J. 2001. *What I've Learned Leading a Great Company and Great People*. London: Headline Book Publishing.

Zolin R, Kropp F. 2008. Public or Private by Genetics of Design?: A Case Study of Organizational Design Decisions for New Public Ventures, *The International Public Management Review (IPMR)* 9, no. 1: 130–147.

Zolin R, Kropp F. 2009. *How Environmental and Organizational Complexity Affects Opportunity Recognition in Development Projects*. CINet. http://eprints.qut.edu.au/27165/1/CINet_09_-_Zolin.pdf

Zolin R, Kropp F. 2010. How Environmental and Organizational Complexity Affects Opportunity Recognition and Exploitation in Development Projects. *Proceedings of the 7th AGSE International Entrepreneurship Research Exchange*. 2–5 February. University of the Sunshine Coast. Queensland.

CHAPTER 3

# Entrepreneurs Dynamically Innovating

When considering the impending era of development that will be the Fourth Industrial Revolution (Schwab 2016; Schwab and Davis 2018), we can base it upon the past or anticipate the future industrial progression, where each revolutionary cycle is as potentially relevant as each manufactory cycle is to each other; and yet the past is gone, and the future unknown. We have, however, defined opportunity across time, to potentially extend into other forms. These may be industrial revolutionary cycles based upon steam, electricity or semi-conductors. These all in their time offered undiscovered opportunity, incrementally or transformational to radical. Those successful ultimately implemented, through experimentation and application, are on a rolling contemporary platform towards realisation in the market, society or environment.

What, therefore, in terms of the transitional progression between the revolutionary cycles, is the cusp of this change?

Change is led by an avant-garde movement and keen intent, ever forming and changing, to quickly (relatively) become the norm, and soon the past, absorbed into the cultural, economic and human societal fabric that overlays our communities. This is so, whether localised, national or global, and increasingly outside the bounds of this planet towards extension across the emergent millennium to planetary systems, galaxies and greater exploration and examination of the universe.

For the exploratory company established at the long tail of the third revolutionary cycle, as cusp to the fourth, the change was not immediately



G. A. Reed, *Entrepreneurs Navigating a Universe of Disruption*,
https://doi.org/10.1007/978-981-19-0703-6_3

evident, including such distinct and defined categories. Rather, the experience was one of crumbling domains, and a diminishing opportunity as markets fragmented dramatically, almost akin to a war of attrition where a gain is seemingly made, in terms of ground or territory claimed, only to find that the front is now very differently defined; the territory has been lost regardless of a supposed victory, which is now deemed pyrrhic; such was the engagement with the market in the screen documentary sector domestically in Australian and global contexts, as it transitioned to factual entertainment. We, as a company of exploratory capacity and resultant *parabolic scramble* framework, worked in terms of our flexible response to changes in the market and circumstances. In hindsight, which is always a seemingly easy evaluation, the *parabolic scramble* framework was the exploratory company's strategically interpretive response to disruption and engagement with a market enduring profound changes.

It was re-assuring to have such a dynamically responsive framework as a concept, and yet from the contemporary position of reflection, and informed with knowledge of the forthcoming revolution of the quantum computing era, the framework was a distilled expression of disruption, though not delineated at the time of its discovery and inception. For, who can really see the future? It is now possible to reflect on the waves of disruption that consumed our resources. In terms of fiscal and physical, we were invested and committed. Everything indicated that we should continue and go forth, at each distinct stage, so accordingly we went. It was just that we would not achieve our goal, as despite a range of indicators, the mechanisms that could and would support our survival in such a disrupted environment, were ultimately exhausted in terms of fiscal, physical and emotional fortitude.

The transition to other objectives would be resultant, so at the end of the iterative cycle it would prove to be fruitful through the struggles and tribulations, however not as initially conceived or contemplated. Casualties would be incurred, in terms of personal losses, and those of more profound cadence. To note, the iterative results of developing documentary and factual programming for broad and narrowcast, akin to most entrepreneurial endeavours, deliver very different end products, one an innovative Australian history series contemporaneously in production for the national Australian broadcaster during the writing of this text, the other, a range of projects engaging with CMR. The alternative narrative and factual storytelling applications utilising an applied version of lean manufacturing, as derived from the Toyota Production System, minimised waste, as transmuted to lean methodology (Ries 2011), and to an applied version for the creative producer, or entrepreneurial producer, perhaps in preference, as a possible *new lean*.

As we move to a global citizenship, we also plan a move off-Earth, first stop the Moon (NASA 2019) to establish a base there in order to have a Mars shot, so building upon the Moon shot of 21 July 1969, that would become legendary in the context of space exploration and achievement. Contemplating the laws of space (maritime/admiralty/treaty), we must also consider the ethical transparency of a joint human-centred endeavour, as too would the leading technology companies on Earth rally to achieve a status of co-operation in preparation for the Fourth Industrial Revolution, and the design and planning of the quantum computing realm (Schwab 2016; Schwab and Davis 2018).

This unique understanding is developed conceptually by advances in technology and its representations in society, both in contemporary terms and historically, as now being built upon towards transformational innovations and design.

As the framework of the *parabolic scramble* emerged, there were applications that became evident in terms of other formats. One that became apparent was that it could offer some conceptual clarity in dynamic, seemingly chaotic environments, such as political and social human centres, whether regional or national, especially in terms of geopolitical movements during the early era of this millennium.

In dynamic environments of disruption, as depicted in recent conflicts across the globe, there can be seen a developing movement to order, as state and non-state actors acclimate to this redefined order and adapt. This is not new. There were similar acclimations during other historical eras, including ancient to the modern; and typically, the experiment was with tactical responses to a stimulus in kinetic environments, and was incrementally acted upon, typically through this continuing experimentation.

In recent conflicts, human-centred design (Kilcullen 2013, 2015) has been utilised in terms of a strategy to good effect, by engaging with urban populations and involving them in security outcomes for their communities. The stakeholders/actors are unified in their desire for security and combine to effect change. It is iterative and somewhat evident after the event, however, not typically before. In terms of recent conflicts, numerous military interventions were enacted before a human-centred design was initiated with communities. Akin to other conflicts, illustratively that of 1914–1918, many combined systems were perfected from being static to the eventual movement of forces, being used formatively in a contemporary context.

In an age of disruption, we may not know future outcomes, however, when we involve the stakeholders, investors, clients, customers, end-users in the process, the outcome is typically built fit-for-purpose. The *parabolic scramble* is one option during a period of disruption to gain clarity when information needs to be processed quickly and with a delicate responsiveness to the seemingly chaotic or to path-dependent extremes. In the case of the stasis of status quo versus the elasticity of nimbly required adjustments, where does the entrepreneurial enterprise invest its slender resources? The answer is to draw in information as readily as is possible, to disseminate expediently and with efficiencies of process and operation, not to mention an evolving strategic engagement, respond as per the *parabolic scramble* framework, literally in-situ.

Key to the defined era of disruption, which is unravelling the socio-political geographic communities within and without national domains, is the opportunity it presents in terms of redefinition. Redefinition is the *parabolic scramble*, its concept extending to any area of disruption, whether human, environmental, kinetic or other. Form is the political act and, as with the example of recent conflicts, the formation of society should entail the involvement of its members with a mutual beneficial investment on the part of those building the society that they want to have. We defer to a governmental structure as amorphous and, much like the current keep-cup when purchasing beverages, not requiring a disposable container in some markets, we may feel we have assisted the environment by doing our part. We may also feel we have completed our citizenry obligation of responsibility by voting at an election, and yet, there is much more that can be done in both cases.

The disruption continues, and we need to learn to redefine human society to be holistic and respectful of other elements of the world, including all biological entities and, importantly, the planetary formations that create such diverse and complex environments. We either value these for their intrinsic contribution to the balance of biological and earthen ecosystems, or disrupt them to the effect that they are irreparably diminished or destroyed. Redefining this era is the responsibility of those who are invested in the opportunity that is being presented to humanity at a juncture of sustainability. If managed and led with vision and strategy, the opportunity will be the inspiration of a new epoch, a heightened human-led era that is respectful and incorporating of all earthly elements. We have the opportunity to do less harm, and to provide for sustaining life on this planet. We must contemplate correctly how we might venture forth as societies, responsibly. Bioplastics and polymers could be introduced as alternatives to current waste plastics that do not bio-degrade. An innovative start-up sector that could provide a range of benefits to human societies and the environments we share with other organic forms is highly desirable.

Time is important. It is good to have the ability to reset and go over events all again, such as in cyclical scenarios, the ability to repeat and learn from the planning, action and reflection, as in religious contexts in terms of redemptive processes, or in popular narrative tales whereby the main character, and associated characters, relive 24 hours (*Groundhog Day* 1993), or a period of time (*Russian Doll* 2019), in order to improve and find a balance, harmony or victory (*Edge of Tomorrow* 2014).

The time that we have is seemingly organised. Yet, it is not so, except as night becomes day across a solar cycle, whereby we as a planet spin through space and time at hundreds of kilometres an hour, depending upon where on the planet you are situated. The hour is a construct of clock time, or an industrialised time period, as the actual concept of time can change. For the *parabolic scramble* framework, the consideration is whether the time for the entrepreneur, exploratory company, company, business, entity or individual has decelerated, or accelerated, to potentially be static or stopped, to then possibly start again, or over. This fits into an iterative format. However, for the *parabolic scramble,* its very bonded area is path dependent potentially and chaotic concurrently. It is simply how the actor wishes to interpret and utilise it.

## Chaos Theory

It became evident after developing the framework of the *parabolic scramble*, that chaos theory would be necessary as a comparison for a full appreciation of the framework (Levy 1994). The *parabolic scramble* is informed by chaos theory and its attempts to derive order from perceived disorder. With reference to screen production and the market that it operates within, and as with any market that may appear to be ad hoc or potentially disordered, chaos theory suggests there is always a pattern (Stewart 1989). Therefore, for my journey there was a reachable understanding of order, no matter what the variables (Burns 2002, 42–44; Gleick 1987, 86).

Margaret Ward outlines in *Butterflies and Bifurcations: Can Chaos Theory Contribute to Our Understanding of Family Systems?* (1995), systems with complex variables and the prediction possible due to their rules of operation. Essentially, Ward explains that there are two parts to Chaos Theory, otherwise called complex dynamical systems. One fundamental aspect of Chaos Theory is that there is actually order to be found in supposed chaotic systems, while, on the other hand, apparently disordered systems ultimately self-organise. Ward cites examples such as the weather or stock market that appear to be unpredictable, when, in reality they possess the elements imposed by nature and environment to produce predictable patterns and therefore order (629–638).

Chaos theory was developed from experiments in 1961 by Edward Lorenz (1917–2008) who was a meteorologist interested in weather prediction (Stewart 1989, 141). These developments were informed by foundational advances by Alan Turing (1912–1954) (1952), the theoretical and practical originator of computer science (1937) and artificial intelligence (1950), Boris Belousov (1893–1970), Robert May (*The Secret Life of Chaos* 2010) and dramatically by Lorenz's *Butterfly Effect* (1972) amongst others, going back to earlier influential works provided by Henri Poincaré (1854–1912) (1890) and Jacque Hadamard (1865–1963) (1898).

It is of relevance to the research investigation that Benoit Mandelbrot (1924–2010) (1977, 1982) was studying cotton prices when he established a previously unobtainable symmetry of the data (Gleick 1987, 86), which, in tandem with chaos theory, lent itself to an understanding of the *parabolic scramble* in relation to a range of applications, whether market-related or otherwise relevant to Remo Media/Reed Films' development or operation. Benoit Mandelbrot (1977, 1982) defined self-similarity as fractals and used the phenomenon to discover the 'fingerprint of nature', performing much of his groundbreaking work whilst employed at IBM (International Business Machines) (*The Secret Life of Chaos* 2010).

With an understanding of entropy (Shannon 1948), as derived from the second law of thermodynamics (Baranger 2001; Haddad et al. 2005), chaos theory becomes potent in its appropriateness for use as background in order to appreciate the qualities of the *parabolic scramble.* If chaos possesses order within its variables in the form of patterns (Gleick 1987; *The Secret Life of Chaos* 2010), entropy is its counterbalance in that it is premised upon the fact that systems are in a constant state of decline or decay and therefore move towards disorder (Baranger 2001). If systems are constantly seeking balance although seemingly chaotic (*The Secret Life of*

*Chaos* 2010), entropy proposes a counter to such order or harmonious state as it represents the potential for destruction of the system (Baranger 2001).

Entropy (Shannon 1948) enables an appreciation that not all systems achieve a static plateau of balance, but rather are dynamic and alive and therefore incorporate decline, or death, according to the range of potential variations. The revelatory conclusion Baranger offers in the paper *Chaos, Complexity and Entropy* (2001) is that in seeking to understand entropy in relation to chaos and complex systems, we must accept its subjectivity and that of our own. Entropy should provide qualitative security. However, Baranger suggests and demonstrates that this is not always the case (16–17).

Chaos theory provides insight through its interpretative qualities and in relation to the *parabolic scramble* its value is that it gives perspective to the dynamics of variables within a context that presents order through patterns (Gleick 1987, 86). The proposed framework I called the *parabolic scramble* as my interaction with the scramble crossing was dealt with parabolically (Block et al. 2006; Galilei 1914; Hooke 1675) on the occasion, that I documented in the journal for the research study, on the 14 October 2008 at 10:28 a.m. I broadened the scope of this framework to include a range of applications in the context of a scramble crossing (Barnes 1965, 103–117) and chaos theory to not only inform but redefine and predetermine a desirable outcome achieving an uninterrupted crossing (Liebowitz and Margolis 1995a, b), assuming that there is a uniform mode of engagement with the crossing.

The chaotic collision of actors in the scramble crossing is a constant. However, order is maintained despite instruction on the use of the crossing not being present and the variables or pedestrians are left to find order through self-organisation (Ward 1995), without the establishment of set rules of engagement. In essence, any movement is possible and yet there are consistent, predictable patterns that have variation but follow set parameters.

## Game Theory

Game theory can also assist with the interpretation of the *parabolic scramble* in the context of screen production (*American Experience: A Brilliant Madness* 2002; Levy 1994, 170–173).

The notion of a metaphorical interpretation that is qualitatively relevant is outlined in the quote below. It is another helpful tool to interpret the *parabolic scramble* and place it into a context with confidence that it exists alongside a milieu of theoretical counterparts. The quote is included to provide context which has assisted the development of the *parabolic scramble*.

Garth Saloner discusses the use of frameworks in relation to game theory in *Modelling, Game Theory, and Strategic Management* (1991), effectively suggesting its qualitative benefits as an intuitive metaphorical device,

> *Almost all development of theory has been via broad conceptual frameworks, verbally reasoned arguments, ... the conceptual framework captured in Porter's (*1980*) 5-forces model has been both influential and useful.... (119–136)*

Game theory was significantly advanced by John Forbes Nash (1928–2015) who developed the Nash Equilibrium. He suffered from schizophrenia throughout his life and demonstrated considerable insight by creating a multifaceted concept with practical applications. Nash assumed an approach to mathematics that operated from the top down which was unconventional, and he refused to be influenced by the work of others, enabling him to achieve the Nash Equilibrium whilst a student at Princeton University (*American Experience: A Brilliant Madness* 2002).

In his doctoral dissertation on *Non-cooperative Games*, Nash (1950a) cites the influential works of John Von Neumann (1903–1957) and Oskar Morgenstern (1902–1977) (1944), which colleague and friend Avinash Dixit explains Nash built upon to develop the Nash Equilibrium (1950a, b, 1951) and concludes,

> *What game theory does is to unify and systematize ... intuitions. Then the general principles extend the intuitions across many related situations, and the calculation of good strategies ... is simplified. (American Experience: A Brilliant Madness* 2002*)*

Game Theory is drawn into a modern application through the *prisoner's dilemma* game as outlined by Matthew Mason in the book *The Pirate's Dilemma: How Youth Culture Is Reinventing Capitalism* (2008, 232–234) which dealt with then contemporary issues surrounding the use of online sources and the Internet (Currah 2006; Gates and Hemingway 1999; Reynolds 2006; Surratt 2001; Turow 1984).

To achieve a mathematical interpretation is desirous; however, not essential for the purposes of this enquiry as it is the metaphorical nature of the interaction that is of interest. How does the metaphor lend use and how can it be incorporated into the structure of Remo Media/Reed Films in its search for interactivity with local, national and global markets?

To entertain the notion of a theoretical plane beyond the requirements of this enquiry is to envisage the purely mathematical and metaphorical nature of an example like game theory (Saloner 1991). There is another that is pertinent and has become important to this book and the *parabolic scramble* framework, being the Mandelbrot set (Mandelbrot 1977, 1982). Its interpretation of fractal geometry in the context of the natural world as it extends through all elements of organic terrestrial existence, and is found in multiple areas, is incredibly significant to the experiences relayed in terms of the scramble crossing and the resultant *parabolic scramble* framework (Taylor et al. 1999).

## The Mandelbrot Set

The importance of the search for order in chaos, as is the objective of chaos theory, is seen to be drawn together in the development of the Mandelbrot set. The Mandelbrot set as depicted in Fig. 3.1 was made possible with the advent of computers that could mass data to divide it to derive its elemental composition and thereby discover a base structure which is termed and represented by the Mandelbrot set (Gleick 1987; Mandelbrot 1977, 1982).

This was a particularly relevant juncture for the *parabolic scramble* with relation to creativity and innovation (Frederick et al. 2013) in the context of this investigation of SME screen production businesses operating from a regional entry position with relation to local, national and global markets (Jackson and Court 2010; Office for the Arts, DPMC 2011, Screen Australia 2010). The Mandelbrot set demonstrates the 'fingerprint of nature' (Mandelbrot 1977, 1982) as illustrated in the work of Jackson Pollack (1912–1956) and represented through geometric fractals (Taylor et al. 1999). There is a leap of faith (Morley 2013) one must take when developing creative works as Jackson Pollock's career demonstrates. His works are numerous and often their provenance contentious. This is where geometric fractals have been used to identify and authenticate his work.

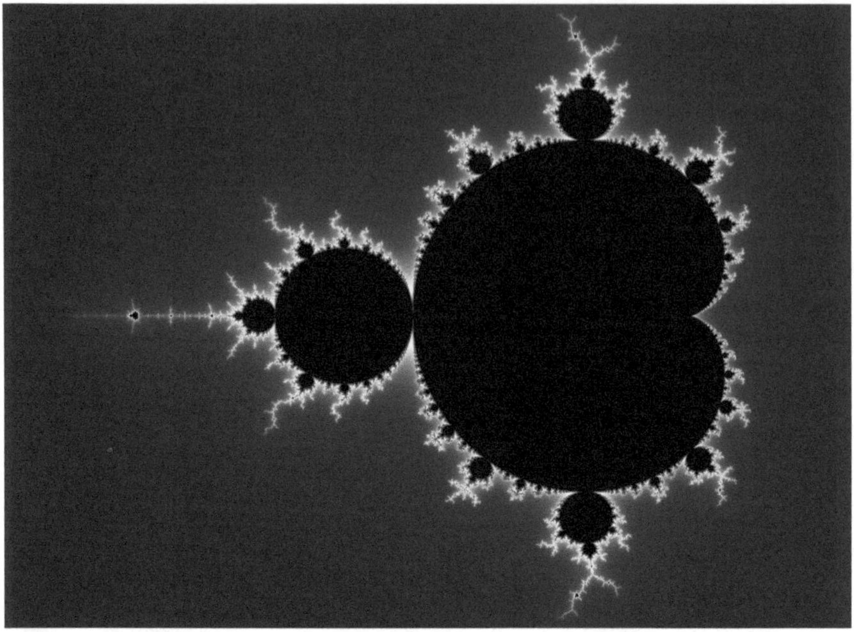

**Fig. 3.1** Mandelbrot set as depicted by physicist Dr Wolfgang Beyer (2006)

Jackson Pollack died before chaos and fractals (Mirowski 1990) were discovered in the context of the Mandelbrot set (1977, 1982) and his paintings demonstrate that at a sub-conscious level Jackson Pollack's art consistently expresses the phenomena of fractal mathematics (Taylor et al. 1999) and chaos theory (Mirowski 1990, 289–307).

The remarkable nature of the Mandelbrot set is that it is a mathematically essential structure in the natural world, through geometric fractals, and for the composition of organic structures (Taylor et al. 1999). Pure mathematical enquiry requires creativity, which, combined with the Mandelbrot set, supports the *parabolic scramble* framework. The *parabolic scramble* is a device of exploration that transcends a purely metaphorical search for information. For Remo Media/Reed Films the advent, and incorporation, of the *parabolic scramble*, to process an organisational structure, is both insightful and purposeful.

Philip Mirowski describes Benoit Mandelbrot in *From Mandelbrot to Chaos in Economic Theory* (1990) as 'stunningly original', especially with regard to his work with 'fractals' which was unorthodox. Mirowski also makes the point that Mandelbrot was fortunate to gain academic freedom at a company like IBM where they allowed him to 'follow his instincts' (289–307).

## Bibliography

American Experience: A Brilliant Madness. 2002. PBS Television. Television program transcript. Arlington. http://www.pbs.org/wgbh/amex/nash/filmmore/pt.html.

Baranger M. 2001. *Chaos, Complexity, and Entropy: A Physics Talk for Non-physicists.* Center for Theoretical Physics, Laboratory for Nuclear Science and Department of Physics. Cambridge: Massachusetts Institute of Technology. http://necsi.edu/projects/baranger/cce.pdf.

Barnes HA. 1965. *The Man with the Red and Green Eyes: The Autobiography of Henry A. Barnes, Traffic Commissioner, New York City.* New York: E P Dutton & Co.

Beyer W. 2006. *Mandelbrot Set: Initial Image of a Zoom Sequence.* Created using the program Ultra Fractal 3. Wikimedia Commons. http://commons.wikimedia.org/wiki/File:Mandel_zoom_00_mandelbrot_set.jpg.

Block P, Dejong M, Ochsendorf J. 2006. "As Hangs the Flexible Line: Equilibrium of Masonry Arches." *Nexus Network Journal* 8, no. 2: 13–24. http://web.mit.edu/masonry/papers/block_dejong_ochs_NNJ.pdf.

Burns J. 2002. "Chaos Theory and Leadership studies: Exploring Uncharted Seas." *Journal of Leadership and Organisation Studies* 9, no. 2: 42–56.

Currah A. 2006. "Hollywood versus the Internet: The Media and Entertainment Industries in a Digital and Networked Economy." *Journal of Economic Geography* 6, no. 4: 439–468.

Frederick H, O'Connor A, Kuratko DF. 2013. *Entrepreneurship: Theory, Process, Practice.* 3rd ed. Melbourne: Cengage.

Galilei G. 1914. *Dialogues Concerning Two New Sciences.* Trans H Crew, A De Salvio and A Favaro (intro). New York: The Macmillan Company. https://oll.libertyfund.org/title/galilei-dialogues-concerning-two-new-sciences.

Gates B, Hemingway C. 1999. *Business @ the Speed of Thought: Using a Digital Nervous System.* New York: Warner Books.

Gleick J. 1987. *Chaos-Making a New Science*. Middlesex: Penguin Books.

Haddad W, Chellaboina V, Nersesov S. 2005. *Thermodynamics: A Dynamical Systems Approach*. Princeton: Princeton University Press.

Hooke R. 1675. *A Description of Helioscopes, and Some Other Instruments*. Printed for John Martyn, Printer to the Royal Society at the Bell in St. Paul's Churchyard, London.

Jackson, P, Court, D. 2010. "Review of the New Zealand Film Commission." A Report to the Hon Chris Finlayson, MP, Minister for the Arts, Culture & Heritage. Wellington.

Kilcullen D. 2013. *Out of the Mountains: The Coming Age of the Urban Guerrilla*. Authors at Google. https://www.youtube.com/watch?v=tVUI9U4WQ6E.

Kilcullen D. 2015. *Out of the Mountains: The Coming Age of the Urban Guerrilla*. Victoria: Scribe.

Levy D. 1994. "Chaos Theory and Strategy: Theory, Application, and Managerial Implications." *Strategic Management Journal* 15, no. 2: 167–178.

Liebowitz S, Margolis S. 1995a. Path Dependence, Lock-in, and History. *Journal of Law, Economics, and Organization* 11, no. 1: 205–226.

Liebowitz S, Margolis S. 1995b. "Policy and Path Dependence: From QWERTY to *Windows* 95." *Regulation: The Cato Review of Business & Government* 18, no. 3: 33–41.

Lorenz EN. 1972. "Predictability: Does the Flap of a Butterfly's Wings in Brazil Set off a Tornado in Texas?" American Association for the Advancement of Science, 139th Meeting. Sheraton Park Hotel, 29 December. http://eaps4.mit.edu/research/Lorenz/Butterfly_1972.pdf.

Mandelbrot B. 1977. *Fractals: Form. Chance and Dimension*. New York: W H Freeman and Company.

Mandelbrot B. 1982. *The Fractal Geometry of Nature*. New York: W H Freeman and Company.

Mason M. 2008. *The Pirate's Dilemma: How Youth Culture is Reinventing Capitalism*. New York: Free Press.

Mirowski P. 1990. "From Mandelbrot to Chaos in Economic Theory." *Southern Economic Journal* 57, no. 2: 289–307.

Morley P. 2013. *Poetry and the Romani Culture*. ABC Radio National: Late Night Live, 2 April.

NASA. 2019. *NASA's Moon to Mars Plans, Artemis Lunar Program Gets Fast Tracked in 2019*, NASA, https://www.nasa.gov/press-release/nasa-s-moon-to-mars-plansartemis-lunar-program-gets-fast-tracked-in-2019.

Nash J. 1950a. "Non-cooperative Games." PhD Thesis. Princeton: Princeton University. https://rbsc.princeton.edu/sites/default/files/Non-Cooperative_Games_Nash.pdf.

Nash J. 1950b. "Equilibrium Points in N-Person Games." *Proceedings of the National Academy of Sciences* 36, no. 1: 48–49.

Nash J. 1951. "Non-cooperative Games." *The Annals of Mathematics* 54, no. 2: 286–295.

Poincaré H. 1890. Sur le problème des trois corps et les équations de la dynamique. Divergence des séries de M. Lindstedt. *Acta Mathematica*, no. 13: 1–270.

Porter ME. 1980. *Competitive Strategy.* New York: Free Press, Macmillan.

Reynolds G. 2006. *Army of Davids: How Markets and Technology Empower Ordinary People to Beat Big Media, Big Government, and Other Goliaths.* Thomas Nelson: Nashville Tennessee.

Ries E. 2011. *The Lean Startup: How Today's Entrepreneurs Use Continuous Innovation to Create Radically Successful Businesses.* New York: Random House.

Saloner G. 1991. "Modeling, Game Theory, and Strategic Management." *Strategic Management Journal* 12, no. 52: 119–136.

Schwab K. 2016. *The Fourth Industrial Revolution.* New York: Random House.

Schwab K, Davis N. 2018. *Shaping the Future of the Fourth Industrial Revolution.* New York: Crown Publishing Group.

Screen Australia. 2010. Submission to the Australian Government's 2010 Review of the Independent Screen Production Sector. Australian Government Screen Australia.

Shannon CE. 1948. A Mathematical Theory of Communication. *The Bell System Technical Journal* 27, no. 3: 379–423.

Stewart I. 1989. *Does God Play Dice? The Mathematics of Chaos.* Middlesex: Penguin Books.

Surratt, CG. 2001. *Internet and Social Change.* North Carolina: McFarland & Company.

Taylor R, Micolich P, Jonas D. 1999. *Can science be Used to Further Our Understanding of Art?* University of New South Wales. Physics World. October. http://authenticationinart.org/pdf/literature/Fractal-Expressionisme-Can-Science-Be-Used-To-Further-Our-Understanding-Of-Art.docx.pdf

The Secret Life of Chaos. 2010. Television program. SBS (Television) on Demand, Sydney. 17 July 2013.

Turing A. 1937. On Computable Numbers, with an Application to the Entscheidungsproblem, *Proceedings of the London Mathematical Society.* Series 2 42, no. 1: 230–265.

Turing A. 1950. Computing Machinery and Intelligence. *Mind* 59, no. 236: 433–460.

Turing A. 1952. The Chemical Basis of Morphogenesis. *Philosophical Transactions of the Royal Society of London. Series B, Biological Sciences* 237, no. 641: 37–72.

Turow J. 1984. *Media Industries: The Production of News and Entertainment.* New York: Longman.

von Neumann J, Morgenstern O. 1944. *Theory of Games and Economic Behaviour.* Princeton: Princeton University Press.

Ward M. 1995. Butterflies and Bifurcations: Can Chaos Theory Contribute to our Understanding of Family Systems? *Journal of Marriage and Family* 57, no. 3: 629–638.

CHAPTER 4

# The Continuing Journey into the Unknown Universe

It is through the augmentation of the *parabolic scramble* that a conceptual understanding and an instantaneous development-in-action can be seen and acted upon in the moment, or with an almost instantaneous reflective, or reflexive quality, to operational and strategic learning, because it is really positioned at the cusp of learning.

The augmentation of reality is able to be technologically enhanced through an increasing plethora of MR or CMR applications. However, this is not the augmentation as a baseline to be detailed here. To augment reality, the *parabolic scramble* is enabling of a perspective of difference for the actor in the midst of its dynamic and spatial operations, lending in recent applications towards the inclusion of the dimension of time, being the fourth-dimensional representation as seen in Fig. 4.1.

To reiterate, it is the very nature of augmentation of the *parabolic scramble* that provides a conceptual understanding, as the instantaneous development-in-action is visible, and through action in the moment; or with an almost instantaneous reflective, or reflexive quality, to operational and strategic learning, because it is really positioned at the cusp of learning.

For the organisation, the *parabolic scramble* framework is a method by which it is possible to conceptualise, plan, strategise and train for the unexpected, or unknown, rather than warn against failure, or educate entrepreneurs to embrace it as the norm. 'Failure' as a term can be reframed, without the necessity to lionise or mythologise those who have supposedly 'failed', the objective being to equip the entrepreneur, or



G. A. Reed, *Entrepreneurs Navigating a Universe of Disruption*,
https://doi.org/10.1007/978-981-19-0703-6_4

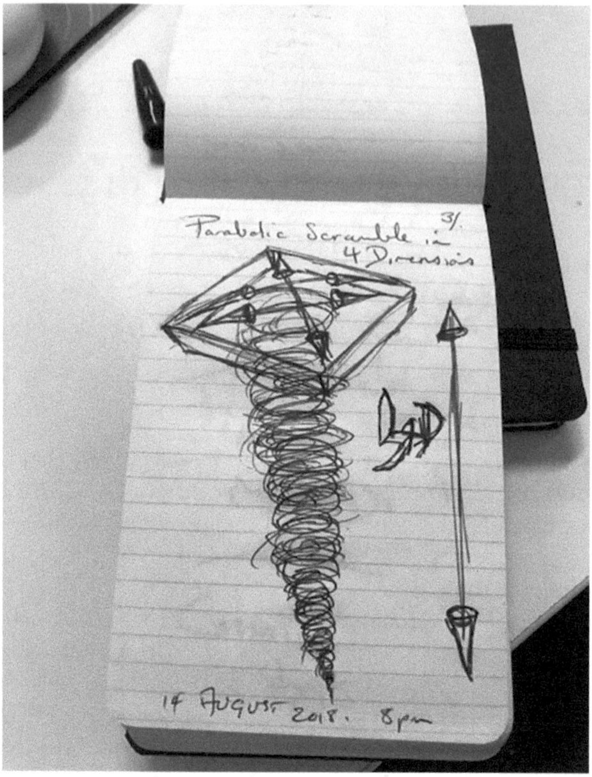


**Fig. 4.1** *Parabolic scramble* in four dimensions as sketched. (Photograph and drawing by Author)

entrepreneurial organisation, intrapreneur, entrepreneur yet to be or otherwise invested or interested, with the ability to learn to succeed in the unknown world of 'risk' by ameliorating to significantly reducing it.

Robust innovation is required as we progress as a society towards a disrupted future of innovation (Juma 2019), whether emergent megatrends (OECD 2018) or other substantive developments in societies globally. As I am writing this text, we are experiencing a global pandemic which has led to a range of distinct innovations, especially in the way we develop and learn in a future-focused environment. As I convert materials and teach my classes, both undergraduate, and postgraduate, I am dealing with and teaching iterative approaches to produce, service, experience and ways in which to deal with 'risk' and 'failure'. I may be dealing with enterprise and entrepreneurial endeavour, from the art meets business perspective of design thinking; however, in an educational context, there have been, and will be, distinct moves to find innovative pedagogies to encompass the ability to be resilient with supposed 'failure' or non-successful outcomes, or, more importantly, the 'risk' that is necessary to learn and experiment, to begin and improve cycles of learning and development.

Importantly, and insightfully on the point of iterative testing, the *parabolic scramble* enables the entrepreneur or entrepreneurial organisation to learn in a muscular context to encounter and deal with change. As with any muscle, it can be developed through exercise and usage. The augmentation of reality is key to the *parabolic scramble* framework, both conceptually and in practice. In itself, the *parabolic scramble* framework is flexible and adaptive for the user. It currently can be utilised as any other framework or tool that can be applied and implemented, from electronic, or written worksheets, to practical exercises for teachers in-class or visually as a depiction that incorporates real-world action or over-layered visual augmentations.

As the framework developed from within an exploratory and emergent company, guided by a research study on the entity, and its interactions with market, founders, contractors, clients, stakeholders, audience or users, it was embedded in the very structure of its engagement with a socially economic environment. The co-founders were actively engaging with fragmenting screen markets, and seeking opportunity, and, much like any venture, it was forthcoming in ways that were not evident at the various stages of interaction across the myriad of interactions with the market and the social-economic environment.

## The Shimmer of Memory

On returning to the Screen Forever conference in Melbourne, Australia, conducted by Screen Producers Australia (SPA), as a session producer for SPA on behalf of the Australian Film Television and Radio School (AFTRS), I realised the benefit of the many conference hours spent in meeting areas of the Crown Metropol and Promenade as an independent producer, whereby interest from potential investors in screen content was initiated. It is a market, and a distinct environment, that has an important business and social context in terms of how to gain interest in projects in development, or otherwise.

When I asked my co-founder to reflect upon the times we spent in those meeting areas and rooms advancing projects, the response was a memory of stressful periods of time and encounters, which they were in part. However, I reflected that they were also part of a process that we, and everyone there seeking to develop projects and secure interest, were engaged in. For my co-founder, the *parabolic scramble* always made sense in terms of conceptualising the business, path dependency, engaging with risk and especially recovering quickly from obstructions, obstacles or the producer's *Yes* or *No* (the second-best response to get from any investor, or interested party is a definite *No*).

## The Kindness of Knowing

The kindness of the *No* was always of benefit because it enabled the re-allocation of resources, and in a sense that is what the *parabolic scramble* embodies, the way to deal with the risk of a venture and the nuance of *Yes*, *No* and *Maybe*. As I patrolled the rooms of the Screen Forever conference seeking to meet with colleagues, former acquaintances, recent contacts or those I hadn't met yet, the shimmer of memory across these seemingly challenging environments was one of incremental to transformational, to radical improvement or development. What was rewarding about attendance at the conference and the interactions that were facilitated there was that they were all contributory to the advancement of the screen producer, content maker's career, because it was the bedrock network, as essential to any entrepreneur, entrepreneurial endeavour or enterprise, that was formed there.

The multitude of projects over the years was the iterative devices, embedded deeply in another iterative cycle that had been building social capital in terms of networks (O'Connor and Reed 2015a, b), and so on and on. The *parabolic scramble* was a perfect representation of this, and these interactions, though not evident or obvious to most individuals embedded in the action. My co-founder always did see it, though, and articulated it often, and to the strategic benefit of current screen projects, or interactions with the market, co-developers, companies, businesses, administration tasks, really a range of endeavour, both social and economic, or other.

As we criss-crossed the carpeted lobbies of the conference areas, moving between floors frequently, there were many opportunities that emerged surprisingly. There were the pitches that went incredibly well where interest was evident from the first greeting, and additional communication was superfluous, to the very unusual, most memorable when attending international markets where the terrain was significantly changed. Of note is a pitch to a US cable network where I was informed by a vice president that they were seeking programmes on extra-terrestrials and those who tracked them. Or producers could be asked for a factual programme with high stakes in what is termed jeopardy (or ideally for this type of television, life and death scenarios, which notably was to be an audience perception and not literal).

Factual entertainment became the area as documentary production changed to provide historical to contemporary information through entertaining formats of several episodes to multiple series as packages (preferred for programming considerations by broadcasters). This was an important moment for the exploratory company as it moved, with the assistance of the *parabolic scramble*, in the market both nationally and internationally. With the reflection of a co-founder who now produces factual non-scripted content across multiple episodes as an original format, the long road of those many meetings and pitches in those rooms and corridors at the differing locations determined a suitable blend of product in the market. However, as with anything original, a rarity and somewhat remarkable in the Australian market where tested formats from overseas are typically purchased and re-purposed for local audience and viewership, there is a risk for executives who back innovation or experiment in the market.

For broadcasters, there is the uncertainty of the new, not only with the concepts and financing but also with every element of a dynamic production across numerous locations, in numerous states, contending with logistics as well as unknown events. One insurmountable issue would present, on the production of one episode in the series, with the casting smoke from bushfires that subdued the visual representation of Sydney Harbour. It was so profoundly engulfing of the location and production team that for work, health and safety (WH&S) reasons the set had to be shut down and the crew dispersed to be re-assembled after the smoke had cleared.

For the producer of factual content in fragmenting markets, the long list of variables and unforeseen eventualities requires the ability to adjust and re-adjust, re-assess and re-purpose. For this application, the *parabolic scramble* is now backgrounded, as the producer may do this instinctively, or not. The most challenging element of any production is that the challenges do not stop; they simply continue. The producer is the driver across the life cycle of the production from conception to delivery to realisation in the market through distribution to a developing maturity, which may encompass re-versioning, re-purposing or re-vitalising as the opportunity or circumstances present.

This is crucially relevant for anyone involved in business and leadership and as positioning enterprise expectant of future disruption across the cycles of change inherent with any developing, or industrialised process. As Remo Media transitioned over time to Reed Films, so too would the iteration continue, or in terms of the developing cycle transition to a new enterprise entitled Refutured, which will encompass new technological applications across the screen and audio/sonic realm. On departure from Reed Films co-founder, Dr Vanna Morosini, successfully launched Flying Kite Pictures securing the original self-generated and developed format series, *Are You Tougher Than Your Ancestors?* for television with Australia's national broadcaster, ABC, which has been recognised with an Australian Academy of Cinema and Television Arts (AACTA) nomination and an Australian Teachers of Media (ATOM) award for Best Factual Television Series.

## The Life-Cycle of Enterprise

The cycles of exploration for the company will continue, as will the cycles of the industrialised revolution now continuous over centuries of human economic endeavour, and with both there is the opportunity to design how we progress. And design should be at the forefront. The culture that is developed and continues will also require thought and consideration during the throes of economic survival, development, growth and maturity. It is the responsibility of those who create to be accountable for their creations, as well as the impact of those creations upon human and non-human society, animate and non-animate, for they are the extension of an organic process that continues.

For the founders of the exploratory company, the changing terrain of the screen broadcast, and narrowcast environment, can only present the need for a *parabolic scramble* implementation and appreciation, for scrambling is what is articulated. Actions that may once have been described by *pivot* now have to be described in a way that shows the disruption. Scrambling seems to be the way to reactively deal with disruption, as seemingly preparation for its exigencies is impossible. Yet the concept of the *parabolic scramble* has been inbuilt and existent for over a decade of the application of the exploratory model. The model has taken the pounding of the unknown to now to know somewhat the scope of reaction needed to ultimately be proactive. For it is not without robust experiment that we learn what not to do, and then what to do.

In much the same way as current video games skill players through re-spawn and iterative successes and non-successes, so too does the *parabolic scramble* in its implementation embody this. The ability to conceptualise chaos, variables, the unknown, uncertainty, time differences, warps, bends, stasis, demonstrates that it can never be known in comfort. All effort regarding significant change and disruption must exist in the uncomfortable zones of fear, learning and growth, for we cannot remain in our comfort zone, and expect to develop, learn and build, take agency or action. This may extend to policy, social, economic, legal, security, societal or any of the myriad of applications in human and non-human contexts and involvements.

David Kilcullen (2014) details participatory co-design and the use of how might we [(HMW) as referencing design thinking concepts] inform consumer connected start-ups solving problems of urban population, security, sanitation and a range of issues. Kilcullen and team offer pathways through disruption to discover alternatives such as collaborative mapping software, working with community groups to address security and safety for urban environments and informal cities, '... bloggers, community television and radio stations, citizen journalists, tech start-ups, design firms all working ...' connectivity, communicate with one another ' ... to understand their ... environment ... communicate with each other to understand the set a list of priorities they need to be addressing ... and this is where the hope lies ...' (Kilcullen 2014).

Consumer electronics can be used to understand the urban environment and its problems—urban overstretch, crime, sanitation—how might we do it differently? To become resilient, to utilise resources effectively, and with direction and purpose to deal with the identified problem through solutions.

So too can be seen in this era of the Fourth Industrial Revolution a re-calibration if we choose to see it as such, whereby there is so much disruption that there can be nothing else except a re-evaluation of the past to connect with the present moment, and project into the future context.

How will we create the structure, organisation and institutions to develop and manage the Fourth Industrial Revolution? How will we become more efficient and eliminate waste and reduce harmful practices to the environment and ourselves?

## Contextualising Disruption

The *parabolic scramble* framework is a means by which disruption is contextualised as a continuum of dynamic movement. We could choose to see it as change, however, and importantly change is the constant. We simply move with it, and do so as part of that continuum. When we really examine the notion of change, and our place in it, we are highly skilled and adapted to be at one with it, as we are in it, and it is by its nature in us (and this is the foundational underpinning of the *parabolic scramble*). We may reminisce about minor detail in terms of the relatively recent past, or a different era; though on both accounts it is immaterial, for we do not possess the past, and cannot. We can, though, possess the present, in order to put in place the mechanisms of structure, organisation and institution as will enable the coming era to be influentially defined, as we do have this capability.

We can iteratively learn from the experiences of the past and experiment into the future. With the best of intentions, there will still need to be adjustments, and modifications, as the terrain changes, and incrementally to transformationally or in some cases radically alters the outcome, whether process, product, service, experience or other. The choice to embrace the coming era, and learn from our disrupted present, is the valuable opportunity of learning; and in this context, the *parabolic scramble* has been informative and useful to determine a state of constant movement and change, especially in terms of the perceived bonded area, and additionally across time, as understood and appreciated with all its variants.

There is an incredible opportunity in the coming revolutionary era, opportunity to correct and learn from the iterations of previous industrial, social, political and historical revolutionary cycles. For this opportunity to be realised, like any other in terms of entrepreneurial endeavour or enterprise, there is a range of implementations that need to be considered, none more so than the stewardship necessary towards the vision of what is wanted from this opportunity. If left to the forces of the economy, without consideration of social, environmental, political, moral and ethical tenets, it is likely that there will be a repeat of the past in terms of cyclical iterations, as that is what is known, and as a species, we build upon that foundation.

However, with knowledge and pro-social behaviours that inform innovation and innovative practices, it is possible to craft this future to not be so industrial in nature, but one in tandem with the natural world and its environment. Nothing says that we need to be cycling through revolutionary industrial cycles, or defined in this modality. As a human species, nothing says we need to be industrious. We may be complementary by alternative, in the building of our shelters, and by addressing our needs as required, and not by massing resources [to hoarding (Smil 2019)] in order to be wealthy as individuals, or nations, for all we essentially require is to meet our needs, and ensure that this is the means by which we exist. It does not need to be survival-based, but instead can be needs-based. For we orientate to survival to get by, and amass the means to be protected in this context, and yet, what we really need does not require the mass of infrastructure often. We are always able to simplify, and streamline the process, review it and reduce waste, much as was done with lean methodology (Ries 2011) off the back of lean manufacturing and the Toyota Production System. Assistance can be delivered to those as they need, when needed, in an efficient and streamlined mode.

In terms of what this next iteration will present, and our part in it, the oppositional process of construction and deconstruction has potential as a format. However, given the organic nature we contribute, do we proceed through the life cycle and accept growth, maturity and decline? Or do we consider over-the-horizon possibilities, such as blue ocean strategy theoretical positions, whereby we look beyond the obvious? We look to the undiscovered or underdeveloped areas where there is no oppositional process required, as it is as we define it, not defined through our desire to be different from what is already existent.

In oppositional political positions there can be checks and balances; however, there is the possibility for consensus, which is outward-looking and exploratory, to developmentally growing, that is importantly not defined by what is, but instead by what can be. There is no need to struggle over the present status quo or resources, because the perspective is one of being originally defined and creating something anew, not repurposing or repositioning the existent. As detailed by forward projections, such as OECD Space and Innovation (2016) or OECD Megatrends and Innovation in Pedagogy (2018), there exist already modes and methodologies to deal with risk, innovation, future study and the means by which to teach those requiring the skills and experience to get there.

How do we achieve this new perspective unencumbered by the thinking, social structures, politics, power dynamics or other?

Perhaps we may be defined by this quest to discover the new, that which is not yet known because we have not gone there. We haven't experienced that uncertainty; however, we embrace it, because that is where we are able to be driven by the excitement of the emergent, the intangible, the magical, the spiritual, the new reason, the new normal, or perhaps the new abnormal, or non-normative.

For if we are disputing power dynamics and representation, we become reductive, not to negate inequality in terms of this representation, for it is the duty of the state to the citizen to provide safety. This extends to all points of inclusivity. Across spectra of potential differences, we include this diversity, for we are already diverse and in this is the richness of organic existence and potential for innovation and its outputs. Distraction from a phenomenon that already exists is to move to a reductive grouping that then seeks to assert a new normal, which is effectively to be abnormal. We are actually abnormal in our individual difference, which is the richness of life. We need the new abnormal to create the new normal, which is thereby to be considered normative. It must be noted that normative behaviour or representations do not typically represent all behaviours or alternatives in society.

When we are considering how we would like the future to be influenced by our foresight, as much as that is possible, and our current knowledge and position, cognisant that it will change substantially in the unknown and as yet unforeseen future. What could be the basis that it is constructed upon?

When evaluating the cycles of industrial revolutions, there are a range of historic periods that are indicative, and present warnings as to what can eventuate if we do not consider the morality and ethical positions upon which we construct our decisions and organise societies. In the last century, there was a culmination of social, political, ideological and economic imperatives present at the juncture of industrialisation, and the formulation of what can become a holocaust, Shoah or crimes against humanity (Robinson 2012). When we consider the potential of our actions as human citizens in the era of industrialisation, we may, through reflection and determination, insulate the next revolutionary cycle from this profound knowledge and collective human experience; for, we as humans do share it as our combined history on this planet. Given the planet Earth is approximately 4.5 billion solar years old, and human archaeological evidence is

100,000 to 200,000 solar years old, our current recorded civilisation is relatively recent. As we face a planet that is in crisis, what will we do innovatively to steer a corrected course? For much like any action into the unknown, we must constantly re-assess and re-determine our path. It is iterative and in order for steerage across the next millennia, our guidance should be informed by morality and ethics to determine the best course.

## Morality and Ethics

The need for morality and ethics (Hursthouse 1999, 2013) when facing challenges to society, and within society, is profound, and there is no greater default, for as human citizens we hold a responsibility to other human citizens, beyond cultural nationalism or cultural normative behaviours.

We may in the context of business enterprise become familiar with strategic business analysis with (Reeves et al. 2015) Porter's Five Forces, Seven Domains, PEST or PESTLE, SWOT, Blue Ocean Strategy, as tools or frameworks. These are some that I regularly teach in the context of Master of Business Administration (MBA) and adapted courses that can be applied as and when we need them, as each tool has its specific purpose. When in need of a rake to score a garden bed or collect fallen leaves, we do not use a spade or a shovel, as we could do, because the rake would be the most efficient or appropriate for the task at hand. As a species, human societies create, in most instances, tools to greater and greater effect, towards AI, ML, CMR and quantum computing applications that will be as we wish them to be and utilised. It is a great opportunity to effect and assert morality, ethics and formulate a clean and clear ecology, to build truth into the ecosystem we desire for all living and non-living entities.

For entrepreneurial endeavour, there have emerged tools and frameworks to accommodate also, and there are those that can be utilised for the raising of a start-up, to deal with the elements needed to scale a business enterprise when resources are limited or non-existent in some instances. However, much like a selection of tools that become familiar for specific and general tasks, the more we become skilled in their usage, the better the application and precision of the result. To know a tool, be instructed in its usage, and then perfect its application is the point to raise here, as I introduce specifics regarding the *parabolic scramble* framework.

The *parabolic scramble* framework is currently being implemented iteratively which is also defined by its nature, and for those using it, there are important inbuilt considerations in terms of criteria. The continuing research regarding its application for educational contexts is a future research direction that is currently underway, and will form an extension of this text and the discussion presented here.

As a child visiting Australia's capital city, Canberra, I watched on loop *The Day the Earth Stood Still* (1951) at the National Library of Australia. The impressive narrative of this cinematic presentation was poignant during an escalating period of Cold War tension during the first part of the 1980s as I moved into the teenage years of questioning and learning about the future that I was to inhabit. Yet, through a range of phenomena human devised, be it weaponry, socio-politic, economic or viral, it seemed there was not to be a stable version of this future possible. *The Day the Earth Stood Still* would be revisited in 2008, though without the bite that those early years of human obliteration seemed to herald during an emergent adulthood so keenly provided in terms of an end-point of civilisation.

Science fiction interested me and informed future thinking during this time with such cinematic offerings in terms of *Bladerunner* (1982), to later be incorporated into and enhanced during *Bladerunner 2049* (2017), perfected as exploratory and experimental in *Ex_Machina* (2014), and as remarkably depicting the sonic realm in the rendering of AI as self-identified in *Her* (2014). Then there was the animated *Alita: Battle Angel* (2019) as a sample progression of cinematic representations of the AI progression conceptually, morally and ethically. There are other depictions of AI through literature, scientific investigation notably towards technological outputs. However, it is the cinematic that informs the mass market conceptually as almost a subjective to objective preparation for what is possible and to come.

*Metropolis* (1927) by Fritz Lang pioneered the representation of AI in the depiction of the cyborg designed to replace the socio-economic political revolutionary figure of Maria in the narrative incorporating Bauhaus, Dada, Art-Deco representations towards the expressionistic cinematic rendering of the subject. There is now the possibility to realise the fiction of science in an even more profound and precise way, with technological capabilities that are exponentially increasing and adaptive.

When implanting the *parabolic scramble* framework into a process, or processes, it is important to consider, as noted earlier, the range of other frameworks that have been developed as tools to be utilised.

Ethical considerations are increasingly the focus across markets, as the consumer base realises the impactful nature of consumption, and, more importantly, the self-reflected and self-referenced consumption of the consumer (Frederick et al. 2019). They can be rapacious and ravaging of all that is exploitable whether animal, vegetable, mineral or any other category.

The important point to be made about disruption as different to innovation is that disruption replaces the old, be it technological, social, societal, political, economic, … ad infinitum.

Include political partisan divisions and disillusionment, bi-partisanship, tri-partisanship, quad-partisanship … ad infinitum? What of a more consensual, invested human-centred alternative that moves beyond the polarised positions of interest groups, whether based upon commercial, social, societal, physical or other advancement or gain? What if we are mindful and truly inclusive across a culture that recognises differences and strives to accommodate the interests and desires of all citizens for the betterment of the society? For then, we move beyond the competitive, adversarial political arena into the fertile new areas that are yet to be discovered or determined. Let us discover new alternatives by seeking to develop our culture, beyond the human-centred to include a living and profoundly productive environment that supports life, and our lives in all its remarkable combinations and diverse forms. The new may not be that new, as it just may be seen for the first time by eyes for which it is a discovery.

The *parabolic scramble* was developed organically from the processes, tangible and intangible, from within a firm (Penrose 1955, 1959). The contribution builds upon those that have gone before and are relevant to their era, and purpose (Reeves et al. 2015). However, in the field of entrepreneurship, which is building its own distinct applications, rather than borrowing from others, there is a developing independence and distinct forms of framework emerging, as also is theory (Frederick et al. 2019).

The *parabolic scramble* as a framework is a tool of understanding during a period of disruption. It is able to be utilised by anyone wishing to engage with this era. It is easy to implement conceptually, physically and culturally across practice or organisations, be it business-orientated or otherwise.

## Forming the Future

We do not know the future; however, we are in receipt of stark information that there needs to be significant to profound change if we are to survive as a species, in communion with the rich diversity of other species and forms on this planet. The previous revolutionary cycles of the bygone industrial ages are our inheritance in all their magnificence and all the destructive by-products of such an accelerated advance across what is but a speck of time in that rich human history, remarkably diminished in terms of the rich geological history of the planet; and yet this relatively minuscule period of geological time has been transformational to all that we now know, and experience as a species. What is the future for, if not to be excited by it and prepare for its advent? How we will construct the coming technological, societal, economic, environmental age is our responsibility and the legacy we bequeath to that future.

## Bibliography

Frederick H, O'Connor A, Kuratko, DF. 2019. *Entrepreneurship: Theory, Process, Practice.* 5th Asia-Pacific ed. Melbourne: Cengage Learning Australia.

Hursthouse R. 1999. "Virtue Ethics and Human Nature." *Hume Studies* 25, nos. 1 & 2: 67–82.

Hursthouse R. 2013. "Virtue Ethics." In E N Zalta (ed). *The Stanford Encyclopedia of Philosophy* (Spring Edition). http://plato.stanford.edu/cgi-bin/encyclopedia/archinfo.cgi?entry=ethics-virtue.

Juma C. 2019. *Innovation and its Enemies: Why People Resist New Technologies.* New York: Oxford University Press.

Kilcullen D. 2014. "A Future of Coastal Connected Cities." TedX Sydney. https://www.youtube.com/watch?v=_AD4c2Rl1l1w.

O'Connor A, Reed GA. 2015a. *Promoting Regional Entrepreneurship Ecosystems: The Role of the University Sector in Australia.* Australian Centre for Entrepreneurship Research Exchange (ACERE). The University of Adelaide, Adelaide, 3–6 February.

O'Connor A, Reed GA. 2015b. *South Australia's Entrepreneurial Ecosystem: Voice of the Customer Research Report.* South Australia Department of State Development. Government of South Australia, Adelaide.

OECD. 2016. *Space and Innovation.* Paris: OECD Publishing. https://doi.org/10.1787/9789264264014-en.

OECD. 2018. *The Future of Education and Skills. Education 2030.* Paris: OECD Publishing http://www.oecd.org/education/2030-project/teaching-and-learning/learning/megatrends/

Penrose E. 1955. "Research on the Business Firms: Limits to Growth and Size of Firms." *American Economic Review* 45, no. 2: 531–543.

Penrose E. 1959. *The Theory of the Growth of the Firm.* New York: John Wiley & Sons.

Reeves M, Haanaes K, Sinha JK. 2015. *Your Strategy Needs a Strategy: How to Choose and Execute the Right Approach.*

Ries E. 2011. *The Lean Startup: How Today's Entrepreneurs Use Continuous Innovation to Create Radically Successful Businesses.* New York: Random House.

Robinson G. 2012. *Crimes Against Humanity: The Struggle for Global Justice.* London: Penguin Books.

Smil V. 2019. *Growth: From Microorganisms to Megacities.* Cambridge, Massachusetts: MIT Press.

CHAPTER 5

# The Use of the *Parabolic Scramble* Framework

Utilising the *parabolic scramble* framework at the pre-start-up phase enables the user to begin the process of defining the (1) culture, (2) vision, (3) pathway, (4) flexibility, with an ability to deal with (5) change and (6) time, each through the prism of 'Values, Ethics, and Personality'.

This is notably an iterative process, and this important aspect has been incorporated into the functionality of the framework and as detailed below (Appendix B).

## Entrepreneurial Culture Creation

At each stage of one iterative, or interacting *parabolic scramble* cycle, the six elements are considered in terms of:

| | |
|---|---|
| Values | baseline morality and developed concepts |
| Ethics | social interaction with colleagues, stakeholders, investors, networks, clients, customers, end-users yet to be defined |
| Personality | persona that will become understood in the market/environment and is a reflection of the founder/s values and ethics through implementation. |


G. A. Reed, *Entrepreneurs Navigating a Universe of Disruption*,
https://doi.org/10.1007/978-981-19-0703-6_5

## Entrepreneurial Culture

Forming the culture of an organisation, which is yet to be, is established with the first movement made towards the nascent enterprise or endeavour. It begins before the first communication is sent out, or the first contact is made with outside parties.

Such a culture is created by the founder, or co-founders, by their values and ethics towards what will become the personality of the enterprise. As such, a consciousness of what this might be into the future is the consideration, and much like establishing, the planning of a future entity can be clearly defined towards its implementation at a conceptual level; and it is suggested that this very orientation is its formulation and foundation. As such the movement towards establishing the culture of an organisation by its originators, at its nascent origins, is instructional to what will be developed into the future life of the enterprise.

It is important to also mention here that there is the possibility of defining an existent culture, to potentially redefine it, or make alterations to its current embedded pathways. This may carry an inheritance of past values and ethics, though can be informed through iterative cycles by new perspectives and implementations towards what will become the revitalised personality of the organisation.

## Entrepreneurial Vision

For the entrepreneur navigating a universe of disruption, the leadership, whether personal, organisational or other across a range of environments, requires a strategic vision. Once equipped with this important directive, the process of planning for eventualities is able to be achieved.

When using the *parabolic scramble* framework, the requirement is to creatively imagine an endpoint based upon research, which, though distinct to that time, will inform the future position and through iteration can be altered incrementally. Such iterative understanding is an assistance to the founder or co-founders maintaining the strategic vision as additional research or experiences develop foundationally for the organisation.

## Entrepreneurial Ecosystem

When contemplating an entrepreneurial ecosystem, and as this becomes reductive to subsections or sectors, it is important to contemplate the organisation's position in the greater context of an array of activities and their systems.

This can entail mapping the entrepreneurial ecosystem, which has been done effectively in a range of localities, such as the AEE. However, what was notable from the research we conducted in Adelaide regarding its start-up support systems was that participants we interviewed had their own pathways. These pathways were to those who used them the mode by which they had developed into the structure of the ecosystem. It was a very organic development typically, though a consciousness of other options as alternate pathways were not necessarily known to the interviewee. When a map of the ecosystem was presented, they could see how they were part of the greater whole. This was when the localised knowledge of the participant became informed by the greater context of an entrepreneurial ecosystem and was not only revelationary but also empowering cognisantly and practically.

## Entrepreneurial Pathways

The entrepreneurial pathways are defined as non-path dependent, and this is achieved through an examination, and clear understanding, of the existent pathways across markets, areas of operations or environment whether bonded or non-bonded.

As can be seen in Figs. 5.1a, 5.1b, and 5.1c the entrepreneurial pathway, as represented in the framework of the *parabolic scramble*, can be different to that of the established pathway as has existed historically, or is perceived to be the most efficient or effective mode of interpreting the environment.

The notion of alternative pathways is understood in the context of path dependency, which may have been the most efficient pathway at one time and, as changes in the environment take place, may through legacy be maintained. With the note that in some circumstances the efficiencies of path dependency may be advantageous, though it is proposed that this is not always the case, and for the entrepreneur offers an alternative mode of operation that can potentially be informative and beneficial.

In terms of pre-conceptualising the alternative pathway to those that are path dependent, this is iteratively interpreted through the *parabolic scramble* framework.

**Fig. 5.1a** Alternate interpretation of movement through the *parabolic scramble*. (Image credit:- Sam Javanrouh as developed by Author)

**Fig. 5.1b** Alternate interpretation of movement through the *parabolic scramble*. (Image credit:- Sam Javanrouh as developed by Author)

**Fig. 5.1c** Alternate interpretation of movement through the *parabolic scramble*. (Image credit:- Sam Javanrouh as developed by Author)

## Entrepreneurial Flexibility

The objective of the *parabolic scramble* is to equip the entrepreneur, or those embarking upon entrepreneurial endeavour at any stage, with the purpose of mindful manoeuvrability. To detail further, this engenders an entrepreneurial mindset that is practised and disciplined through iterative cycles to the nuance of change as exists in the market, area of operations or environment across a range of contexts.

## Entrepreneurial Change

Figure 5.2 represents an identification photograph of an incoming prisoner or detainee, and this multi-frame image was taken as I adopted the persona of a prisoner moving through the criminal judicial system. This was in order to convey the experience or point-of-view (POV) of someone involved in the experience of being processed into a prison. The restrictions of the political environment enabled an innovation of style and content that made the result far greater than the scripted prepared documentary.

**Fig. 5.2** Photograph taken at Northfield Women's Prison during the *Straight-talk* documentary production. (Photograph by Author)

As documented in Fig. 5.2, the detainee is instructed to cross their arms diagonally palms facing into their chest and to stand looking forward for the identification photographs. The POV is at this moment looking at the instructing correctional officer providing the direction through the criminal justice system, and at this stage represents its advent for the incoming prisoner, or detainee, being processed into this system of corrections.

As a documentarian and in terms of camera operation and visual capture, there is a distinct innovative quality to the action. And as a reflection of entrepreneurial practice and change regarding behaviour and business, *Straight-talk* as a production across the criminal justice system in South Australia was seminal. As Winston Churchill contextualised it, this was to be the 'end of the beginning', the culmination of an apprenticeship across a range of productions, and projects, as preparation for an entrepreneurial endeavour that became the professional trajectory that commenced at this point and continues to this day.

## Entrepreneurial Time

With regard to industrial time, or the clock time of technology, this can be viewed as quantitative in its incremental delineation of the cycle of one complete rotation of the Earth in space. Alternatively, time can be viewed qualitatively, which includes notions of psychological time as written about by Dr Henry-Louis Bergson (1859–1941) in his doctoral thesis *Time and Free Will: An Essay on the Immediate Consciousness of Data* (2001).

For my father, Wesley, as depicted in Fig. 5.3, during the era when he led a team in the making of clocks at Smiths Industries Pty Ltd., the notion of industrial time was accepted, though complex, as he and his team designed and constructed precision instruments. My father had been responsible for banning the use of the work whistle to denote the working timings for employees, which he viewed as demeaning and disrespectful. Within the constraints of industrial time, or clock time, Wesley demonstrated an acceptance and revulsion of this quantitative mode, whilst employed to make the very devices that measured the passing increments of a solar day.

It was the advent of the camera that enabled chronophotography to capture incremental moments of movement through a time that assisted establishing the notion or consciousness of time. I was introduced to photography at an early age at my school and at the same time was brought up by someone who designed and created clocks with teams. Time was to be viewed through the lens of space, which was also an interest of mine as a child, as the Space Shuttle missions propelled humans outside of a day as

**Fig. 5.3** Passport photograph of Wesley Reed during the 1970s. (Photograph by Author)

represented by the revolution of the Earth in space, which they would observe from orbit.

The unreal becomes real, the unknown known as humanity explores beyond the environment of Earth, and ventures into the very essence of our relationship with time, being in relation to space. Future positioning of the expanse of time includes the flow of time, a stretch of time, that precedes any instance, a multiplicity in the concept of time, not necessarily only comprising the individual elements or incremental components related to a solar cycle. Notably, there is also geological and geospatial time.

For the entrepreneur, time may incorporate quantitative and qualitative elements. The entrepreneur may need to accelerate exponentially to then stop, whilst others continue. For it is suggested much akin to the complexity of time itself, there is a complexity of the relationship an entrepreneur will and must have with the multifaceted notion of time.

## Opportunity Within Disruption

During such a profound human era, and the global response to a pandemic such as COVID-19, the notion of globalisation, with an international focus, and the way that capitalism will progress into the Fourth Industrial Revolutionary cycle, seems to echo Joseph Schumpeter's (1934, 1954, 1961) creative destruction. Though importantly, this notion also aligns with Sarasvathy and Venkataraman (2011), who suggest entrepreneurship to be the method by which the new age will progress, much akin to Francis Bacon and the importance of the scientific method for the First Industrial Revolutionary cycle.

## Results and Implications

The *parabolic scramble* is being utilised in postgraduate courses at the AFTRS, with educators, students and practitioners to formulate enterprises, successfully deriving unique outcomes, but also complementing other business strategy frameworks. These results of the research are being presented as an exploratory case study with real-world applications, not only for the screen and audio sectors but also for other economic sectors, as well as implications for the coming Industrial Revolutionary cycle.

## The Philosophy of Entrepreneurship

For Laine and Kibler (2018), who view entrepreneurship as philosophy, and Hjorth (2014), Hjorth et al. (2015), who note the process of this entrepreneurial philosophical position, the *parabolic scramble* enables its user/s to engage with these important facets with defined reflective and iterative phases.

Building a flexible, pluralist, postmodern organisation upon which the foundation of all future planning, strategic vision outputs in terms of operations, tactics and cultural ethical interactions are formed.

## Reforming the Future

The educator, student or practitioner is able to build from a pre-start-up conceptual undertaking to then implement the framework of the *parabolic scramble* as detailed in Appendix A and B, and in continuing development as an ongoing philosophical process. There is also the added benefit of being able to be applied to disruptive innovation and fragmenting markets, as new global developments are embraced as part of the ongoing change that has moved, and continues to move, what was new to what is now considered to be *normal.*

## Bibliography

Bergson HL. 2001. *Time and Free Will: An Essay on the Immediate Consciousness of Data*. London: Dover Publications.

Hjorth D. 2014. "Sketching a Philosophy of Entrepreneurship." In Baker, T and Welter, F (eds). *The Routledge Companion to Entrepreneurship*. London: Routledge: 41–58.

Hjorth D, Holt R, Steyaert C. 2015. "Entrepreneurship and Process Studies." *International Small Business Journal* 33, no. 6: 599–611.

Laine L, Kibler E. 2018. "Towards a Mythic Process Philosophy of Entrepreneurship." *Journal of Business Venturing Insights* 9: 81–86.

Sarasvathy SD, Venkataraman S. 2011. "Entrepreneurship as Method: Open Questions for an Entrepreneurial Future." *Entrepreneurship Theory and Practice* 35, no. 1: 113–135.

Schumpeter JA. 1934. *The Theory of Economic Development.* Cambridge: Harvard University Press.

Schumpeter JA. 1954. *History of Economic Analysis.* New York: Oxford University Press.

Schumpeter JA. 1961. *The Theory of Economic Development.* Cambridge: Harvard University Press.

# Appendices


G. A. Reed, *Entrepreneurs Navigating a Universe of Disruption*,
https://doi.org/10.1007/978-981-19-0703-6

# Appendix A

# PARABOLIC SCRAMBLE

A research project conducted
by Dr. Gerard Reed

Senior Lecturer of Screen Business
Australian Film Television
and Radio School (AFTRS)
gerard.reed@aftrs.edu.au

## INTRODUCTION

There is need of a framework for entrepreneurial enterprise, and endeavour, that has inherent flexibility and dynamic properties. For the practitioner in the entrepreneurial arena, dealing with uncertainty and risk, amidst economic, technological, and social disruption the ability to conceptualise and engage with change across societal fragmentation is beneficial to business processes. This is especially required in terms of strategizing, planning and the development of the firm, or organisation, as it constructs internal culture and projects that it has a distinct ethos in the market.

## BACKGROUND

With its genesis as a study of an independent screen production company (the exploratory company) this entrepreneurship research is based upon the pioneering investigations of tangible and intangible assets of the firm as discovered during Edith Penrose's mid-twentieth century examination of a firm from within. This pioneering Penrosian perspective provides the theoretical foundation upon which the Parabolic Scramble emerges, from an embedded research study of an enterprise, to demonstrate how the exploratory company develops its organisational learning in the market-place, and the entrepreneurial arena.

## METHODOLOGY

The methodology, in the early stages, utilised action learning research assisted by a grounded theoretical approach, and through the researcher's interactions with a pedestrian scramble crossing in the city of Adelaide, South Australia, the framework of the Parabolic Scramble emerged. The Parabolic Scramble developed adaptively from a conceptual to a practical application for the entrepreneur, entrepreneurial organisation or enterprise, or anyone seeking through organisational learning to follow alternative pathways to an established norm.

## RESULTS

Building upon Edith Penrose (1955, 1959: Penrose & Pitelis, 2009)'s pioneering discovery of intangible assets and the Resource Based View (RBV) of the firm (Barney, 1986a, 1986b, 1991, 2001), the Parabolic Scramble framework was developed from the methodologies of Action Research (Reason, 1988, 1998, 1999, 2003, 2005, 2006) assisted by Grounded Theory (Glaser, 1982, 1998a, 1998b, 1999, 2001, 2005, 2010: Glaser and Holton, 2004: Glaser and Strauss, 1967) and entitled the Parabolic Scramble. The methodology and research are based upon a diagonal or scramble pedestrian crossing (Barnes, 1965)

the Parabolic Scramble enables the entrepreneur (Sarasvathy, 2001, 2010), or those yet to be, a means by which they are able to encounter the unknown, and the associated risks involved with such uncertainty.

Utilising an exploratory case study, removed from the screen sector in which the company was operating, to then freely associate with the entrepreneurial ecosystem in South Australia (O'Connor & Reed, 2014a, 2014b, 2015a, 2015b, 2017), other states within Australia and then internationally. The framework proved to be an effective tool for the exploratory company across a range of economic, network and social applications in a range of markets. The Parabolic Scramble assisted, and informed, the exploratory company as it encountered fragmentation and disruption in these markets. Such a framework is complementary to other tools that maybe utilised such as Design Thinking, Porter's Five Forces, PESTLE, 7 Domains, SWOT, Blue Ocean Strategy however it has an additional benefit in that it has a specific component that enables the user to deal with time as a fourth dimensional element. The notion that entrepreneurial time is different to other formats of time is also made cognisant with the use of the Parabolic Scramble framework.

The detail of there being differing comprehension of time, whether clock, industrial, chronological or other, is incorporated in the Parabolic Scramble, where entrepreneurial time is enabled to accelerate, decelerate,

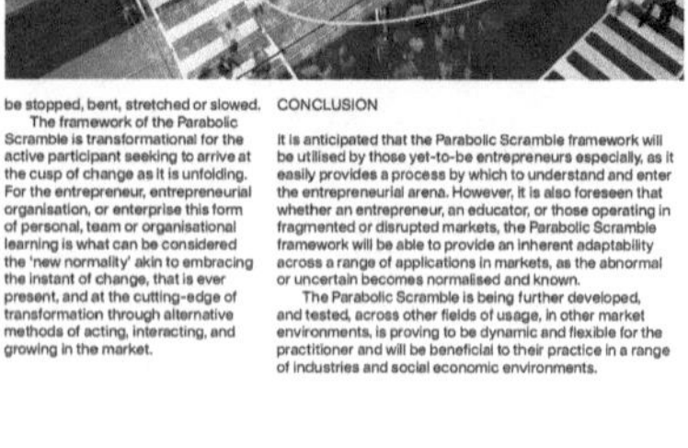

be stopped, bent, stretched or slowed.

The framework of the Parabolic Scramble is transformational for the active participant seeking to arrive at the cusp of change as it is unfolding. For the entrepreneur, entrepreneurial organisation, or enterprise this form of personal, team or organisational learning is what can be considered the 'new normality' akin to embracing the instant of change, that is ever present, and at the cutting-edge of transformation through alternative methods of acting, interacting, and growing in the market.

## CONCLUSION

It is anticipated that the Parabolic Scramble framework will be utilised by those yet-to-be entrepreneurs especially, as it easily provides a process by which to understand and enter the entrepreneurial arena. However, it is also foreseen that whether an entrepreneur, an educator, or those operating in fragmented or disrupted markets, the Parabolic Scramble framework will be able to provide an inherent adaptability across a range of applications in markets, as the abnormal or uncertain becomes normalised and known.

The Parabolic Scramble is being further developed, and tested, across other fields of usage, in other market environments, is proving to be dynamic and flexible for the practitioner and will be beneficial to their practice in a range of industries and social economic environments.

Scanned image: Handwritten process notes made by Gerard Reed.

Photograph: Prepared by Gerard Reed, from a time-lapse photograph by Sam Javanrouh of a scramble crossing at Toronto, Canada.

AFTRS
Australian Film Television
and Radio School

# Appendix B

## PARABOLIC SCRAMBLE FRAMEWORK ANALYSISWORKSHEET

Use this worksheet to perform analysis for case study or real-world application/s.
It is a requirement of this framework that the action is entrepreneurial and innovative in character and implementation.

| COMPANY NAME OR PERSONA | |
|---|---|
| **SUMMARY OF COMPANY HISTORY/IDENTIFIED INDUSTRY/CURRENT POSITION**<br><br>AT EACH STAGE OF ONE ITERATIVE/INTERACTING PARABOLIC SCRAMBLE CYCLE THE SIX ELEMENTS BELOW ARE CONSIDERED IN TERMS OF:<br>• VALUES - (BASELINE MORALITY AND DEVELOPED CONCEPTS)<br>• ETHICS - (SOCIAL INTERACTION WITH COLLEAGUE/S, STAKEHOLDER/S, INVESTOR/S, NETWORK/S, CLIENT/S, CUSTOMER/S, END-USER/S, YET TO BE DEFINED)<br>• PERSONALITY - (PERSONA THAT WILL BECOME UNDERSTOOD IN THE MARKET/ENVIRONMENT AND IS A REFLECTION OF THE FOUNDER/S VALUES AND ETHICS THROUGH IMPLEMENTATION) | |
| **1. CULTURE (That you will develop in your enterprise into the future)** | |
| • Values -<br>• Ethics -<br>• Personality - | |
| **2. VISION (The endpoint that you creatively imagine, or have determined through research)** | |
| • Values -<br>• Ethics -<br>• Personality - | |
| **3. PATHWAY (The known pathway that you will follow, or the pathway you imagine or conceptualize you may discover)** | |
| • Values -<br>• Ethics -<br>• Personality - | |
| **4. FLEXIBILITY (The ability to be responsive to unknown or dynamic factors in an environment or scenario)** | |
| • Values -<br>• Ethics -<br>• Personality - | |

| **5. CHANGE (The incorporated understanding that anticipates changing circumstances constantly and consistently)** | |
|---|---|
| • Values -<br>• Ethics -<br>• Personality - | |
| **6. TIME (The recognition that time is different to people and their cultures, as well as the modes of operation)** | |
| • Values -<br>• Ethics -<br>• Personality - | |

## PARABOLIC SCRAMBLE CONSIDERATIONS

| **1. CULTURE (That you will develop in your enterprise into the future)** | |
|---|---|
| Culture is created and begins with action. The owner of action creates culture. How will relationships be developed? (Team/s, network/s, stakeholder/s, investor/s, partner/s, co-founder/s …) | |
| **2. VISION (The endpoint that you creatively imagine, or have determined through research)** | |
| Vision is the endpoint, now.<br>Where is the endpoint?<br>What is the plan to arrive at the vision/endpoint? | |
| **3. PATHWAY (The known pathway that you will follow, or the pathway you imagine or conceptualize you may discover)** | |
| What is the pathway?<br>What is not the pathway?<br>Where is the pathway? | |
| **4. FLEXIBILITY (The ability to be responsive to unknown or dynamic factors in an environment or scenario)** | |
| Maneuverability through action.<br>Agility with difference. | |

| **5. CHANGE (The incorporated understanding that anticipates changing circumstances constantly and consistently)** | |
|---|---|
| Anticipation of change.<br>Being there with the change, in unison. | |
| **6. TIME (The recognition that time is different to people and their cultures, as well as the modes of operation)** | |
| Is accelerated effort required?<br>Is decelerated effort required?<br>Is it important to wait?<br>Is it important to stop?<br>Is it important to start again? | |

# Bibliography


Alexander C. 2003. *The Bounty*. London: Harper Collins Publishers.

American Experience: A Brilliant Madness. 2002. PBS Television. Television program transcript. Arlington. http://www.pbs.org/wgbh/amex/nash/filmmore/pt.html.

Australian Broadcasting Authority. 2004. *Documentary Guidelines: Interpretation of 'Documentary' for the Australian Content Standard*. Commonwealth of Australia, Sydney.

Australian Film Commission. 2006. Submission to the Department of Communications Information Technology and the Arts: Review of Australian Government Funding Support. Canberra: Australian Government Australian Film Commission.

Australian Taxation Office. 2009. *Producer Offset-Timing of Claims-Liquidation Option*. Australian Government Australian Taxation Office.

Baranger M. 2001. *Chaos, Complexity, and Entropy: A Physics Talk for Non-physicists*. Center for Theoretical Physics, Laboratory for Nuclear Science and Department of Physics. Cambridge: Massachusetts Institute of Technology. http://necsi.edu/projects/baranger/cce.pdf.

Barnes HA. 1965. *The Man with the Red and Green Eyes: The Autobiography of Henry A. Barnes, Traffic Commissioner, New York City*. New York: E P Dutton & Co.

Barney J. 1986a. "Strategic Factor Markets: Expectations, Luck and Business Strategy." *Management Science* 32, no. 10: 1231–1241.

Barney J. 1986b. "Organizational culture: Can it be a source of sustained competitive advantage?" *Academy of Management Review* 11, no. 3: 656–665.




G. A. Reed, *Entrepreneurs Navigating a Universe of Disruption*, https://doi.org/10.1007/978-981-19-0703-6

Barney J. 1991. "Firm Resources and Sustained Competitive Advantage." *Journal of Management* 17, no. 1: 99–120.

Barney J. 2001. "Is the Resource-based 'View' a Useful Perspective for Strategic Management Research? Yes." *Academy of Management Review* 26, no. 1: 41–56.

Barry P. 2009. *Who Wants to be a Billionaire? The James Packer Story.* Sydney: Allen & Unwin.

Berger PL, Luckmann T. 1967. *The Social Construction of Reality.* London: Allen Lane The Penguin Press.

Bergson HL. 2001. *Time and Free Will: An Essay on the Immediate Consciousness of Data.* London: Dover Publications.

Beyer W. 2006. *Mandelbrot Set: Initial Image of a Zoom Sequence.* Created using the program Ultra Fractal 3. Wikimedia Commons. http://commons.wikimedia.org/wiki/File:Mandel_zoom_00_mandelbrot_set.jpg.

Blank S. 2013. "Why the Lean Start-up Changes Everything." *Harvard Business Review.* https://hbr.org/2013/05/why-the-lean-start-up-changes-everything.

Blank S. 2018. *NewTV is the Antithesis of a Lean Startup. Can it work?* https://hbr.org/2018/08/newtv-is-the-antithesis-of-a-lean-startup-can-it-work.

Bligh, W, Bach J, National Library of Australia. 1987. The Bligh Notebook: "Rough account – Lieutenant Wm Bligh's voyage in the Bounty's launch from the ship to Tofua & from thence to Timor", 28 April to 14 June 1789, with a draft list of the Bounty mutineers. Canberra: National Library of Australia.

Block P, Dejong M, Ochsendorf J. 2006. "As Hangs the Flexible Line: Equilibrium of Masonry Arches." *Nexus Network Journal* 8, no. 2: 13–24. http://web.mit.edu/masonry/papers/block_dejong_ochs_NNJ.pdf.

Boreham, G. 2012. *Convergence Review: Final Report.* Department of Broadband, Communications and the Digital Economy (Australia), Australia Government. https://apo.org.au/node/29219

Burchett W. 1977. *Grasshoppers & Elephants: Why Viet Nam Fell.* Urizen Books, Collingwood.

Burns J. 2002. "Chaos Theory and Leadership studies: Exploring Uncharted Seas." *Journal of Leadership and Organisation Studies* 9, no. 2: 42–56.

Calder T. 2011. *Screen Australia Welcomes Funding Increase and Producer Offset Reform.* Screen Australia, 10 May.

Chandrashekar J, Duan Z, Klansky J, Zhang Z. 2005. "Limiting Path Exploration in BGP." 24th Annual Joint Conference of the IEEE Computer and Communications Societies. *Proceedings of the IEEE INFOCOM* 4: 2337–2348, Miami, 13–17 March.

Connolly R. 2008. *Embracing Innovation: A New Methodology for Feature Film Production in Australia.* AFTRS Centre for Screen Business. Canberra: Australian Government Australian Government Australian Film Television and Radio School.

Cooper B, Vlaskovits, P. 2016. *The Lean Entrepreneur: How Visionaries Create Products, Innovate with New Ventures, and Disrupt Markets.* New York: Wiley & Sons.

Cranton P. 1994. *Understanding and Promoting Transformative Learning: A Guide for Educators of Adults.* San Francisco: Jossey-Bass Publishers.

Cranton P. 1996. *Professional Development as Transformative Learning: New Perspectives for Teachers of Adults.* San Francisco: Jossey-Bass Publishers.

Crook A. 2012. "Screen Australia Says No Conflict Over Film Funding." *Crikey.* http://www.crikey.com.au/2012/03/27/screen-australia-says-no-rats-in-our-ranks-over-film-funding/

Csikszentmihalyi M. 1999. "Implications of a Systems Perspective for the Study of Creativity" In R. J. Sternberg (ed.). *Handbook of Creativity.* Cambridge: Cambridge University Press: 313–35.

Csikszentmihalyi M. 2004. "Flow, the Secret to Happiness." Ted Talk. https://www.ted.com/talks/mihaly_csikszentmihalyi_on_flow?language=en#t-918.

Currah A. 2006. "Hollywood versus the Internet: The Media and Entertainment Industries in a Digital and Networked Economy." *Journal of Economic Geography* 6, no. 4: 439–468.

Daly P. 2013. "Towards a City of Entrepreneurs: The Emergence of Adelaide as a Recognised Start-up Community." Paper presented at the Towards a City of Entrepreneurs forum, Adelaide Convention Centre, 25 June.

David P. 1985. "Clio and the economics of QWERTY." *American Economic Review* 75, no. 2: 332–337.

David P. 1986. "Understanding the Economics of QWERTY: The Necessity of History." In W Parker (ed). *Economic History and the Modern Economist.* Oxford: Blackwell: 30–49.

David P. 1994. "Why are Institutions the Carriers of History? Path Dependence and the Evolution of Conventions, Organizations and Institutions. *Structural Change and Economic Dynamics* 5, no. 2: 205–220.

David P. 1997. "Path Dependence and the Quest for Historical Economics: One More Chorus of the Ballad of QWERTY." University of Oxford Discussion Papers in Economic and Social History, no. 20. http://www.nuff.ox.ac.uk/economics/history/paper20/david3.pdf.

David P. 1999. "At Last, A Remedy for Chronic QWERTY-Skepticism!" Working Paper. All Souls College, Oxford University. https://econpapers.repec.org/paper/wopstanec/99025.htm

David P. 2000. *Path Dependence, its Critics and the Quest for Historical Economics.* All Souls College. Oxford: Oxford University.

De Bono E. 1992. *Serious Creativity: Using the Power of Lateral Thinking to Create New Ideas.* London: Harper Collins Business. Imprint of Harper Collins Publisher.

De Bono E. 2016. *Parallel Thinking.* London: Penguin Books.

DeadlineDetroit. 2019. *Mike Duggan Transition Team Quotes Winston Churchill, Gets Quote Wrong*. https://www.deadlinedetroit.com/articles/7285/mike_duggan_transition_team_quotes_winston_churchill_gets_quote_wrong

Deeb G. 2014. "The 4 Types of Entrepreneurs–Which Are You?" *Forbes Online*. https://www.forbes.com/sites/georgedeeb/2014/11/07/the-4-types-of-entrepreneurs-which-type-are-you/ - 3f03fc153e9e

Design Council. 2019. *The Design Process: What is the Double Diamond?* https://www.designcouncil.org.uk/news-opinion/design-process-what-double-diamond.

Dick B. 1997. "Action Learning and Action Research." *Resource Papers in Action Research*. http://www.aral.com.au/resources/actlearn.html.

Drucker PF. 2004. *Innovation and Entrepreneurship*. Oxford: Butterworth-Heinemann.

Einstein A. 1905. "Eine neue Bestimmung der Molecküldimensionen." PhD Thesis. Universität Zürich, Zürich. http://www.pitt.edu/~jdnorton/lectures/Rotman_Summer_School_2013/Einstein_1905_docs/Einstein_Dissertation_German.pdf

Einstein A. 1916. Die Grundlage der Allgemeinen Relativitätstheorie. Annalen Der Physik. Vierte Folge (Fourth Episode). *Band* 49, no. 7: 770–822. http://www.physik.uni-augsburg.de/annalen/history/einstein-papers/1916_49_769-822.pdf.

Einstein A. 1940. "Science and Religion." *Nature* 146, no. 3706: 605–607.

Evatt H. 1955. *Rum Rebellion*. Sydney: Angus & Robertson.

Field M, Golubitsky M. 1992. *Symmetry in Chaos: A Search for Pattern in Mathematics, Art and Nature*. Oxford: Oxford University Press.

Film Australia. 2006. *Review of Australian Government Film Funding Support Submission*. Government of Australia. https://apo.org.au/sites/default/files/resource-files/2007-06/apo-nid15305.pdf.

Frederick H, O'Connor A, Kuratko DF. 2013. *Entrepreneurship: Theory, Process, Practice*. 3rd ed. Melbourne: Cengage.

Frederick H, O'Connor A, Kuratko, DF. 2019. *Entrepreneurship: Theory, Process, Practice*. 5th Asia-Pacific ed. Melbourne: Cengage Learning Australia.

Frith D. 2012. "Joining the Stream of IPTV Promises to Cut Cable and Costs." *The Australian*.

Galilei G. 1914. *Dialogues Concerning Two New Sciences*. Trans H Crew, A De Salvio and A Favaro (intro). New York: The Macmillan Company. https://oll.libertyfund.org/title/galilei-dialogues-concerning-two-new-sciences.

Gammage B. 1974. *The Broken Years: Australians in the Great War*. Canberra: ANU Press.

Gates B, Hemingway C. 1999. *Business @ the Speed of Thought: Using a Digital Nervous System*. New York: Warner Books.

Glaser BG, Strauss AL. 1967. *The Discovery of Grounded Theory: Strategies for Qualitative Research*. Chicago: Aldine Publishing Company.

Gleeson B. 2018. "9 Navy Seal Sayings That Will Improve Engagement and Accountability in Your Organisation." *Forbes*. https://www.forbes.com/sites/brentgleeson/2018/07/11/9-navy-seal-sayings-that-will-improve-engagement-and-accountability-in-your-organization/ - 22ab8b4e6312

Gleick J. 1987. *Chaos-Making a New Science*. Middlesex: Penguin Books.

Haddad W, Chellaboina V, Nersesov S. 2005. *Thermodynamics: A Dynamical Systems Approach*. Princeton: Princeton University Press.

Harris R. 2011. *Question on Notice-enquiry Regarding ABC Programming: FACTory Initiatives Information*. Canberra: Department of the Senate. https://apo.org.au/sites/default/files/resource-files/2011-10/apo-nid26848.pdf

Hawking S. 1988. *A Brief History of Time*. New York: Bantam Dell Publishing Group.

Hjorth D. 2014. "Sketching a Philosophy of Entrepreneurship." In Baker, T and Welter, F (eds). *The Routledge Companion to Entrepreneurship*. London: Routledge: 41–58.

Hjorth D, Holt R, Steyaert C. 2015. "Entrepreneurship and Process Studies." *International Small Business Journal* 33, no. 6: 599–611.

Hooke R. 1675. *A Description of Helioscopes, and Some Other Instruments*. Printed for John Martyn, Printer to the Royal Society at the Bell in St. Paul's Churchyard, London.

Horkheimer M. 1974. *Eclipse of Reason*. New York: Seabury Press.

Hough R. 1994. *Captain James Cook: A Biography*. London: Hodder and Stoughton Ltd.

House of Representatives. 2013. *Tax and Superannuation Laws Amendment (2013 Measures no. 2) Bill 2013*. Parliament of the Commonwealth of Australia. https://www.aph.gov.au/Parliamentary_Business/Bills_Legislation/Bills_Search_Results/Result?bId=r5013.

Howkins J. 2001. *The Creative Economy: How People Make Money from Ideas*. London: Allen Lane.

Hursthouse R. 1999. "Virtue Ethics and Human Nature." *Hume Studies* 25, nos. 1 & 2: 67–82.

Hursthouse R. 2013. "Virtue Ethics." In E N Zalta (ed). *The Stanford Encyclopedia of Philosophy* (Spring Edition). http://plato.stanford.edu/cgi-bin/encyclopedia/archinfo.cgi?entry=ethics-virtue.

Jackson, P, Court, D. 2010. "Review of the New Zealand Film Commission." A Report to the Hon Chris Finlayson, MP, Minister for the Arts, Culture & Heritage. Wellington.

Jaffe E. 2012. "A Brief History of the Barnes Dance." *The Atlantic Cities*. 18 December. http://www.theatlanticcities.com/commute/2012/12/brief-history-barnes-dance/4189/

James J. 1997. *Thinking in the Future Tense*. New York: Touchstone.

James Wilson H, Daugherty P R. 2018. "Collaborative Intelligence: Humans and AI are Joining Forces." Boston: Harvard Business Review.

Jones D, Barlow J, Finlay S, Savage H. 2003. *NZfilm: A Case Study of the New Zealand Film Industry*. Wellington: Competitive Advantage New Zealand.

Juma C. 2019. *Innovation and its Enemies: Why People Resist New Technologies*. New York: Oxford University Press.

Kilcullen D. 2013. *Out of the Mountains: The Coming Age of the Urban Guerrilla*. Authors at Google. https://www.youtube.com/watch?v=tVUI9U4WQ6E.

Kilcullen D. 2014. "A Future of Coastal Connected Cities." TedX Sydney. https://www.youtube.com/watch?v=_AD4c2Rl1i1w.

Kilcullen D. 2015. *Out of the Mountains: The Coming Age of the Urban Guerrilla*. Victoria: Scribe.

Kor Y, Mahoney J. 2004. "Edith Penrose's (1959) Contributions to the Resource-based View of Strategic Management." *Journal of Management Studies* 41, no. 1: 183–191.

Kuhn TS. 1970. *The Structure of Scientific Revolutions*. 2nd ed. Chicago: The University of Chicago Press.

Kuhn TS. 1977. "Objectivity, Value Judgement, and Theory Choice." Reprinted by permission from *The Essential Tension: Selected Studies in the Scientific Tradition and Change*. The University of Chicago Press, Chicago: 356–367. http://www.andrew.cmu.edu/user/kk3n/philsciclass/kuhn.pdf.

Kuhn TS. 1996. *The Structure of Scientific Revolutions*. 3rd ed. Chicago: The University of Chicago Press.

Kuhn TS. 2011. *Stanford Encyclopedia of Philosophy*. http://plato.stanford.edu/entries/thomas-kuhn/.

Laine L, Kibler E. 2018. "Towards a Mythic Process Philosophy of Entrepreneurship." *Journal of Business Venturing Insights* 9: 81–86.

Levin G. 2013. "Jackson Pollock, Lee Krasner and a New Concept of Nature." *Ritsumeikan Studies in Language and Culture* 24, no. 3: 29–37.

Levy D. 1994. "Chaos Theory and Strategy: Theory, Application, and Managerial Implications." *Strategic Management Journal* 15, no. 2: 167–178.

Liebowitz S, Margolis S. 1995a. Path Dependence, Lock-in, and History. *Journal of Law, Economics, and Organization* 11, no. 1: 205–226.

Liebowitz S, Margolis S. 1995b. "Policy and Path Dependence: From QWERTY to *Windows* 95." *Regulation: The Cato Review of Business & Government* 18, no. 3: 33–41.

List D. 2002. *Know Your Audience: A Practical Guide to Media Research*. 3rd ed. Wellington: Original Books.

List D. 2005. "Social Network Mapping: The Development of a Methodology for Social Enquiry." PhD Thesis. The University of South Australia, Adelaide.

Lorenz EN. 1972. "Predictability: Does the Flap of a Butterfly's Wings in Brazil Set off a Tornado in Texas?" American Association for the Advancement of

Science, 139th Meeting. Sheraton Park Hotel, 29 December. http://eaps4.mit.edu/research/Lorenz/Butterfly_1972.pdf.

Mahoney J, Pandian J. 1992. "The Resource-based View Within the Conversation of Strategic Management." *Strategic Management Journal* 13, no. 5: 363–380.

Mandelbrot B. 1977. *Fractals: Form. Chance and Dimension*. New York: W H Freeman and Company.

Mandelbrot B. 1982. *The Fractal Geometry of Nature*. New York: W H Freeman and Company.

Mann S. 2001. "Shackleton's Way: Leadership Lessons from the Great Antarctic Explorer." *Leadership & Organization Development Journal* 22, no. 6: 301–303.

Mannix L. 2013. "Film Corp Has Less Money, But More 'Mouths To Feed'." *Indaily*. 30 January.

Mason M. 2008. *The Pirate's Dilemma: How Youth Culture is Reinventing Capitalism*. New York: Free Press.

Matthews C. 1988. *Hardball: How Politics is Played Told by One Who Knows The Game*. New York: Harper Perennial.

Meagher RE. 2014. *Killing from the Inside Out: Moral Injury and Just War*. Oregon: Cascade Books.

Mezirow J. 1990. *Fostering Critical Reflection in Adulthood*. San Francisco: Jossey-Bass Publishers.

Mezirow J. 1991. *Transformative Dimensions of Adult Learning*. San Francisco: Jossey-Bass Publishers.

Mezirow J. 1995. "Transformative Theory of Adult Learning." In M Welton (ed). *In Defense of the Lifeworld*. Albany: State University of New York Press: 39–70.

Mezirow J. 1996. "Contemporary Paradigms of Learning." *Adult Education Quarterly* 46, no. 3: 158–172.

Mezirow J. 2000. *Learning as Transformation: Critical Perspectives on a Theory in Progress*. San Francisco: Jossey-Bass Publishers.

Mirowski P. 1990. "From Mandelbrot to Chaos in Economic Theory." *Southern Economic Journal* 57, no. 2: 289–307.

*Missing: Presumed Dead*. 2012. ABC Television. http://www.abc.net.au/tv/guide/abc1/201212/programs/DO0725S001D2012-12-19T100001.htm.

Morley P. 2013. *Poetry and the Romani Culture*. ABC Radio National: Late Night Live, 2 April.

Morrell M, Capparell S. 2003. *Shackleton's Way: Leadership Lessons from the Great Antarctic Explorer*. London: Nicholas Brealey Publishing Limited.

NASA. 2019. *NASA's Moon to Mars Plans, Artemis Lunar Program Gets Fast Tracked in 2019*, NASA, https://www.nasa.gov/press-release/nasa-s-moon-to-mars-plansartemis-lunar-program-gets-fast-tracked-in-2019.

NASA Jet Propulsion Laboratory. 1977a. California Institute of Technology. http://voyager.jpl.nasa.gov/spacecraft/goldenrec.html.

NASA Jet Propulsion Laboratory. 1977b. California Institute of Technology. http://voyager.jpl.nasa.gov/spacecraft/images/golden_record_cover.gif.

NASA Jet Propulsion Laboratory. 1997. California Institute of Technology. http://photojournal.jpl.nasa.gov/jpegMod/PIA01081_modest.jpg.

NASA Jet Propulsion Laboratory. 1998. California Institute of Technology. http://photojournal.jpl.nasa.gov/catalog/PIA00317.

NASA Jet Propulsion Laboratory. 2013a. "Voyager: The Interstellar Mission." California Institute of Technology. http://voyager.jpl.nasa.gov/science/bibliography.html.

NASA Jet Propulsion Laboratory. 2013b. "How Do We Know When Voyager Has Reached Interstellar Space?" California Institute of Technology. Media release, September 12. https://www.jpl.nasa.gov/news/how-do-we-know-when-voyager-reaches-interstellar-space

NASA Jet Propulsion Laboratory. 2013c. "Voyager: The Interstellar Mission: Golden Record." California Institute of Technology. http://voyager.jpl.nasa.gov/spacecraft/goldenrec1.html.

NASA Johnson Space Center. 1984. http://www.nasa.gov/multimedia/imagegallery/image_feature_286.html.

NASA Mars Exploration: Program & Missions. 1998. "Mars Pathfinder." https://mars.nasa.gov/programmissions/missions/past/pathfinder/

NASA. 2007. "Voyager to the Outer Planets." NASA Jet Propulsion Laboratory. California Institute of Technology, California.

NASA. 2012. "Voyager: An Interstellar Journey." NASA. http://www.nasa.gov/mission_pages/voyager/index.html.

Nash J. 1950a. "Non-cooperative Games." PhD Thesis. Princeton: Princeton University. https://rbsc.princeton.edu/sites/default/files/Non-Cooperative_Games_Nash.pdf.

Nash J. 1950b. "Equilibrium Points in N-Person Games." *Proceedings of the National Academy of Sciences* 36, no. 1: 48–49.

Nash J. 1951. "Non-cooperative Games." *The Annals of Mathematics* 54, no. 2: 286–295.

Naughton J. 2012. "Thomas Kuhn: The Man Who Changed the Way the World Looked at Science." *The Observer*. http://www.theguardian.com/science/2012/aug/19/thomas-kuhn-structure-scientific-revolutions.

Neale P, Thapa S, Boyce C. 2006. *Preparing a Case Study: A Guide for Designing and Conducting a Case Study for Evaluation Input*. Watertown: Pathfinder International.

Nesheim J. 1997. *High Tech Start Up: The Complete How-to Handbook for Creating Successful New High Tech Companies*. Saratoga, California: Fritz/Brett Associates.

Newton I. 1846. *Newton's Principia: The Mathematical Principles of Natural Philosophy*. Trans A Motte & D Adee, New York. http://archive.org/details/newtonspmathema00newtrich

NSW Government. 2015. "Population Estimates-Australian States, Territories and Capital Cities, 2012." NSW Department of Trade & Investment, Regional Infrastructure & Services.

O'Brien G, Opie J. 2003. "The Multiplicity and Consciousness and the Emergence of the Self." *The Self in Neuroscience and Psychiatry*. Cambridge: Cambridge University Press. Draft October 2000. http://www.adelaide.edu.au/directory/gerard.obrien?dsn=directory.file;field=data;id=12821;m=view

O'Brien R. 1998. *An Overview of the Methodological Approach of Action Research*. Faculty of Information Studies. University of Toronto.

O'Connor A, Reed GA. 2014a. *Innovating for Entrepreneurship in a Regional Milieu/Ecosystem: The Role of the University Sector*. Transatlantic Policy Consortium Conference. Indiana Memorial Union (IMU). Bloomington, 23–24 June.

O'Connor A, Reed GA. 2014b. *Adelaide Entrepreneurial Ecosystem: Policy Design and Program Research Grant Preliminary Report*. South Australia Department of State Development. Government of South Australia, Adelaide.

O'Connor A, Reed GA. 2015a. *Promoting Regional Entrepreneurship Ecosystems: The Role of the University Sector in Australia*. Australian Centre for Entrepreneurship Research Exchange (ACERE). The University of Adelaide, Adelaide, 3–6 February.

O'Connor A, Reed GA. 2015b. *South Australia's Entrepreneurial Ecosystem: Voice of the Customer Research Report*. South Australia Department of State Development. Government of South Australia, Adelaide.

O'Connor A, Reed GA. 2017. *From Helices to Multiverse Theory: Exploring the Diversity Within Entrepreneurial Ecosystems*. University Industry Innovation Network (UIIN). University Industry Engagement – International Asia-Pacific Conference. The University of Adelaide, Adelaide, 15–17 February.

O'Neil B, Raftery J, Round K. 1996. *Playford's South Australia: Essays on the History of South Australia 1933–1968*. Association of Professional Historians Inc., Adelaide.

OECD. 2016. *Space and Innovation*. Paris: OECD Publishing. https://doi.org/10.1787/9789264264014-en.

OECD. 2018. *The Future of Education and Skills. Education 2030*. Paris: OECD Publishing http://www.oecd.org/education/2030-project/teaching-and-learning/learning/megatrends/

Office for the Arts. 2011, 2010. *Review of the Australian Independent Screen Production Sector*. Canberra: Government of Australia Department of Prime Minister and Cabinet.

Olsberg J. 2012. *Building Sustainable Film Businesses: The Challenge for Industry and Government.* https://www.filminstitutet.se/globalassets/2.-fa-kunskap-om-film/analys-och-statistik/publications/other-publications/building-sustainable-film-businesses%2D%2D-the-challenges-for-industry.pdf.

Page B, Potter E. 2003. *The Murdoch Archipelago.* London: Simon & Schuster.

Pajares F. 2013. *The Structure of Scientific Revolutions: Outline and Study Guide.* Emory University. http://www.uky.edu/~eushe2/Pajares/Kuhn.html

Parliament of Australia Commonwealth of Australia. "Inquiry into Recent ABC Programming Decisions: Australian Government's Response to the Committee's Report 2012." Canberra: Parliament of Australia Commonwealth of Australia. https://www.aph.gov.au/Parliamentary_Business/Committees/Senate/Environment_and_Communications/Completed_inquiries/2010-13/abc/index

Pedler M, Burgoyne J. 2015. "Action Learning." In H Bradbury (ed). *The Sage Handbook of Action Research.* London: SAGE Publications: 179–187.

Penrose E. 1955. "Research on the Business Firms: Limits to Growth and Size of Firms." *American Economic Review* 45, no. 2: 531–543.

Penrose E. 1959. *The Theory of the Growth of the Firm.* New York: John Wiley & Sons.

Penrose E, Pitelis C. 2009. *The Theory of the Growth of the Firm.* Oxford: Oxford University Press.

Penrose R. 2011. Uncertainty in Quantum Mechanics: Faith or Fantasy? *Philosophical Transactions: Mathematical, Physical and Engineering Sciences* 369, no. 1956: 4864–4890.

Peters MA, Besley TAC. 2008. "Academic Entrepreneurship and the Creative Economy." *Thesis Eleven* 94, no. 1: 88–105.

Pine G. 2009. *Teacher Action Research: Building Knowledge Democracies.* Thousand Oaks: Sage Publications Inc.

Pitelis E. 2009. *Edith Penrose's 'The Theory of the Growth of the Firm' Fifty Years Later.* Cambridge: University of Cambridge.

Poincaré H. 1890. Sur le problème des trois corps et les équations de la dynamique. Divergence des séries de M. Lindstedt. *Acta Mathematica,* no. 13: 1–270.

Polanyi K. 1957. *The Great Transformation.* Boston: Beacon Press.

Polanyi K. 2001. *The Great Transformation: The Political and Economic Origins of our Time.* Boston: Beacon Press.

Porter ME. 1980. *Competitive Strategy.* New York: Free Press, Macmillan.

Porter ME. 1985. *Competitive Advantage: Creating and Sustaining Superior Performance.* New York: Free Press, Macmillan: 33–38.

Porter ME. 1990. *The Competitive Advantage of Nations.* London: Macmillan.

Porter ME. 1998a. "Clusters and the New Economics of Competition." *Harvard Business Review* 76, no. 6: 77–90.

Porter ME. 1998b. *On Competition.* Boston: Harvard Business Review Press.

Porter ME. 2001. "Strategy and the Internet." *Harvard Business Review* 79, no. 3: 63–78.

Porter ME, Millar VE. 1985. "How Information Gives you Competitive Advantage: The Internet Revolution is Transforming the Nature of Competition." *Harvard Business Review* 63, no. 4: 149–160.

Prest W, Round K, Fort C. 2001. *The Wakefield Companion to South Australian History*. Adelaide: Wakefield Press.

Preston M. 2007. *Movie FX Success No Act*. Smart Company. http://www.smartcompany.com.au/construction-and-engineering/030277-movie-fx-success-no-act.html

Price D. 2008. *The Pixar Touch: The Making of a Company*. New York: Alfred A. Knope.

Prytherch R. 1990. *Harrod's Librarian's Glossary and Reference Book*. Aldershot: Gower Publishing Company.

Puffert D. 2000. "The Standardization of Track Gauge on North American Railways, 1830–1890." *Journal of Economic History* 60, no. 4: 933–960.

Puffert D. 2001. *Path Dependence in Spatial Networks: The Standardization of Railway Track Gauge*. Department of Economics. https://www.sciencedirect.com/science/article/abs/pii/S0014498302907862.

Puffert D. 2002. "Path Dependence in Spatial Networks: The Standardization of Railway Track Gauge." *Explorations in Economic History* 39, no. 3: 282–314.

Puffert D. 2004. "Path Dependence, Network Form, and Technological Change." In W Sundstrom, T Guinnane, and W Whatley (eds). *History Matters: Essays on Economic Growth, Technology, and Demographic Change*. Stanford: Stanford University Pres.

Puffert D. 2009. *Tracks Across Continents, Paths Through History: The Economic Dynamics of Standardization in Railway Gauge*. Chicago: The University of Chicago Press.

Puffert D. 2010. *Path Dependence*. EH.net. http://eh.net/?s=puffert

Rampell C. 2013. "Hollywood's Biggest Bang for its Buck." *The New York Times*. Business Day. *Economix*. 9 August.

Rapp D. 2006. "How 'Star Wars' Surprised the World." *American Heritage*. http://www.americanheritage.com/entertainment/articles/web/20060525-star-wars-george-lucas-movies-hollywood-luke-skywalker-darth-vader-american-graffiti-science

Ratner C. 2002. "Subjectivity and Objectivity in Qualitative Methodology." *Forum Qualitative Sozialforschung / Forum: Qualitative Social Research* 3, no. 3, Art. 16. http://www.qualitative-research.net/index.php/fqs/article/view/829/1800

Reason P. 1988. "Whole Person Medical Practice." In P Reason (ed). *Human Inquiry in Action*. London: Sage Publications: 102–126.

Reason P. 1998. "Co-operative Inquiry as a Discipline of Professional Practice." *Journal of Interprofessional Care* 12, no. 4: 419–436.

Reason P. 1999. "Integrating Action and Reflection through Co-operative Inquiry." *Management Learning Special Issue: The Action Dimension in Management: Diverse Approaches to Research, Teaching and Development* 30, no. 2: 207–227.

Reason P. 2003. "Doing Co-operative Inquiry." In J Smith (ed). *Qualitative Psychology: A Practical Guide to Methods.* London: Sage Publications.

Reason P. 2005. "Living as Part of the Whole." *Journal of Curriculum and Pedagogy* 2, no. 2: 35–41.

Reason P. 2006. "Choice and Quality in Action Research Practice." *Journal of Management Enquiry* 15, no. 2: 187–203.

Reason P Bradbury, H. 2008. *The Sage Handbook of Action Research: Participatory Inquiry and Practice.* London: Sage Publications.

Reason P Torbert, W. 2001. "The Action Turn: Toward a Transformational Social Science." *Concepts and Transformations* 6, no. 1: 1–37.

Reed GSW. 1998. "A Case Study into the Failure of the Team Concept at a Medium Sized Company and What Might be Done to Re-introduce It." Minor Thesis, Master of Total Quality Management (Honours), University of Wollongong.

Reeves M, Haanaes K, Sinha JK. 2015. *Your Strategy Needs a Strategy: How to Choose and Execute the Right Approach.*

Report to the New Zealand Film Commission. 2002. *Scoping the Lasting Effects of The Lord of the Rings.* NZ Institute of Economic Research (Inc.). Wellington & Auckland.

Restivo S. 2005. *Science, Technology, and Society: An Encyclopedia.* Oxford: Oxford University Press.

Revans R. 1980. *Action Learning: New Techniques for Management.* London: Blond & Briggs.

Revans R. 1983. "What is Action Learning?" *Journal of Management Development* 1, no. 3: 64–75.

Reynolds G. 2006. *Army of Davids: How Markets and Technology Empower Ordinary People to Beat Big Media, Big Government, and Other Goliaths.* Thomas Nelson: Nashville Tennessee.

Ries E. 2011. *The Lean Startup: How Today's Entrepreneurs Use Continuous Innovation to Create Radically Successful Businesses.* New York: Random House.

Robinson G. 2012. *Crimes Against Humanity: The Struggle for Global Justice.* London: Penguin Books.

Rosen R. 1985. *Anticipatory Systems: Philosophical, Mathematical, and Methodological Foundations.* New York: Pergamon Press.

Roubiczek P. 1966. *Existentialism For and Against.* London: Cambridge University Press.

Rukstad M, Collins D. 2009. *The Walt Disney Company: The Entertainment King.* Boston: Harvard Business School.

Russell B. 1975. *Power*. London: Unwin Books, George Allen and Unwin Limited.

Russell B. 1976. *In Praise of Idleness.* London: Unwin Books, George Allen and Unwin Limited.

Russell B. 1985. *The Impact of Science on Society.* Hertfordshire: Unwin Paperbacks, George Allen and Unwin Limited.

Russell B. 1987. *A History of Western Philosophy.* London: Unwin Hyman Limited.

Saloner G. 1991. "Modeling, Game Theory, and Strategic Management." *Strategic Management Journal* 12, no. 52: 119–136.

Sarasvathy SD. 2001. "Causation and Effectuation: Toward a Theoretical Shift from Economic Inevitability to Entrepreneurial Contingency." *The Academy of Management Review* 26, no. 2: 243–263.

Sarasvathy SD. 2010. *What Makes Entrepreneurs Entrepreneurial?* The University of Virginia. http://www.effectuation.org/sites/default/files/documents/what-makes-entrepreneurs-entrepreneurial-sarasvathy.pdf.

Sarasvathy SD, Venkataraman S. 2011. "Entrepreneurship as Method: Open Questions for an Entrepreneurial Future." *Entrepreneurship Theory and Practice* 35, no. 1: 113–135.

Sayer-Jones, L. 2014. *Media Law for Non-Lawyers.* Australian second edition, Double Bay: Prêt à Porter Publications.

Scarborough N, Zimmerer T. 2006. *Effective Small Business Management: An Entrepreneurial Approach.* 8th ed. New Jersey: Pearson Prentice Hill.

Schekkerman J. 2006. *How to Survive in the Jungle of Enterprise Architecture Frameworks.* 3rd ed. Victoria: Trafford.

Schumpeter JA. 1934. *The Theory of Economic Development.* Cambridge: Harvard University Press.

Schumpeter JA. 1954. *History of Economic Analysis.* New York: Oxford University Press.

Schumpeter JA. 1961. *The Theory of Economic Development.* Cambridge: Harvard University Press.

Schumpeter JA. 1976. *Capitalism, Socialism and Democracy.* London: Unwin Books, George Allen and Unwin Limited.

Schwab K. 2016. *The Fourth Industrial Revolution.* New York: Random House.

Schwab K, Davis N. 2018. *Shaping the Future of the Fourth Industrial Revolution.* New York: Crown Publishing Group.

Screen Australia Act. 2008, 2013. *Australian Government Com Law*, no. 12 2008. http://www.comlaw.gov.au/Details/C2008A00012

Screen Australia Conflict of Interest Policy. 2010. *Human Resources Policy and Guidelines.* Australian Government Screen Australia.

*Screen Australia Strategic Plan.* 2012-2015, 2012. Australian Government Screen Australia.

Screen Australia. 2008. *Australian Screen Production Incentive: Producer Offset Guidelines.* Australian Government Screen Australia.

Screen Australia. 2010. Submission to the Australian Government's 2010 Review of the Independent Screen Production Sector. Australian Government Screen Australia.

Screen Australia. 2012a. *Documentary: Number and Hours of Australian Documentaries (Not Including Broadcaster-produced Titles) by Location of Production Company, 1997 /98-2011/12.* Australian Government Screen Australia.

Screen Australia. 2012b. *Getting Down to Business: The Producer Offset Five Years On.* Australian Government Screen Australia.

Screen Australia. 2012c. *Offset Loans and Cashflow Providers.* Australian Government Screen Australia.

Screen Australia. 2013a. *Producer Offset.* Australian Government Screen Australia. http://www.screenaustralia.gov.au/producer_offset/.

Screen Australia. 2013b. *Definitions and Specifications.* Australian Government Screen Australia.

Screen Australia. 2013c. *Australian Bureau of Statistics (ABS) Data on Television.* Australian Government Screen Australia.

Screen Australia. 2015a. *Hours of Australian Documentaries (Not Including Broadcaster-produced Titles) by Location of Production Company, 1997/98–2013/14.* Australian Government Screen Australia. https://www.screenaustralia.gov.au/fact-finders/production-trends/documentary-production/activity-summary

Screen Australia. 2015b. *Hours of First-Release Australian Documentaries Broadcast on Free-to-Air TV, 1998–2014,* Australian Government Screen Australia. http://www.screenaustralia.gov.au/research/statistics/releasesdocumentariestv.aspx.

Screen Hub. 2013. *Documentary Stoush (3): Crusaders Storm Email Barricades.* Screen Hub Industry News.

Screen Production Investment. 2013. South Australian Film Corporation. South Australia Government, Adelaide.

Senate Environment and Communications References Committee (SECRC). 2011, 2012. ABC responses to Questions on Notice: Inquiry Into Recent ABC Programming Decisions, 2011, Department of the Senate, Canberra, viewed 16 April 2022. https://www.aph.gov.au/Parliamentary_Business/Committees/Senate/Environment_and_Communications/Completed%20inquiries/2010-13/abc/report/~/media/wopapub/senate/committee/ec_ctte/completed_inquiries/2010-13/abc/report/report.ashx

Sergeant A. 2011. Scrutinizing the Rainbow: Fantastic Space in *The Wizard of Oz* (1939). *Alphaville Journal of Film and Screen Media,* Issue 2. http://alphaville-journal.com/Issue%202/PDFs/ArticlesPDF/ArticleSergeant.pdf.

Shackleton V. 1995. *Business Leadership.* London: Thomson Learning.

Shank GD. 2006. *Qualitative Research: A Personal Skills Approach.* 2nd ed. New Jersey: Pearson Merrill Prentice Hall.

Shannon CE. 1948. A Mathematical Theory of Communication. *The Bell System Technical Journal* 27, no. 3: 379–423.

Shenoy S. 2009 (ed). *A Tiger by the Tail.* The Institute of Economic Affairs and the Ludwig von Mises Institute. Vienna. http://mises.org/library/tiger-tail-0

Sibley B. 2006. *Peter Jackson: A Film-Maker's Journey.* Sydney: Harper Collins Publishers.

Skilton M, Hovsepian F. 2018. *The 4th Industrial Revolution: Responding to the Impact of Artificial Intelligence on Business.* Cham: Palgrave Macmillan.

Sledge EB. 1981. *With the Old Breed: At Peleliu and Okinawa.* New York: Ballantine Books.

Smil V. 2019. *Growth: From Microorganisms to Megacities.* Cambridge, Massachusetts: MIT Press.

Soanes C, Stevenson A. 2004. *Concise Oxford English Dictionary.* Oxford: Oxford University Press.

Soosalu G, Henwood S, Deo A. 2019. *Head, Heart, and Gut in Decision Making: Development of a Multiple Brain Preference Questionnaire.* SAGE Open. https://journals.sagepub.com/doi/full/10.1177/2158244019837439#articleCitationDownloadContainer

*South Australian Film Corporation Act 1972.* Adelaide: South Australian Government. https://www.legislation.sa.gov.au/LZ/C/A/SOUTH%20AUSTRALIAN%20FILM%20CORPORATION%20ACT%201972.aspx.

South Australian Film Corporation. South Australian Film Corporation General Guidelines *2012.* Adelaide: South Australian Government.

South Australian Film Corporation. *South Australian Film Corporation Program Guideline: Special Initiatives The FACTory for Factual Entertainment. 2010.* Adelaide: South Australian Government.

South Australian Film Corporation. South Australian Film Corporation Strategic Review Issues Paper *2012.* Adelaide: South Australian Government.

South Australian Film Corporation. *South Australian Film Corporation Strategic Review Phase 2 2013.* Adelaide: South Australian Government.

South Australian Film Corporation. 2012. "Nick McMahon Breakthrough Producer Award." Media Release. South Australian Film Corporation, Adelaide, 15 November.

Spar DL. 2001. *Ruling the Waves: Cycles of Discovery, Chaos, and Wealth from the Compass to the Internet.* New York: Harcourt Inc.

Spinks P. 2013. Voyager 1 Crosses the Final Frontier. *The Sydney Morning Herald.* http://www.smh.com.au/technology/sci-tech/voyager-1-crosses-the-final-frontier-20130913-2tpe2.html.

Stanford Encyclopedia of Philosophy. 2012a. *Virtue Ethics.* 8 March. http://plato.stanford.edu/entries/ethics-virtue/.

Stanford Encyclopedia of Philosophy. 2012b. *Wilhem Dilthey.* http://plato.stanford.edu/entries/dilthey/.

Steve Jobs: Billion Dollar Hippie. 2011. Television program. ABC Television. 8 October 2014. http://www.abc.net.au/tv/programs/steve-jobs-billion-dollar-hippy/

Steve Jobs Stanford Commencement Address. 2005. Stanford University, California, 14 June. http://news.stanford.edu/2005/06/14/jobs-061505/

Stewart I. 1989. *Does God Play Dice? The Mathematics of Chaos.* Middlesex: Penguin Books.

Stewart JB. 2005. *Disney War.* New York: Simon & Schuster.

Stockings C. 2010. *Zombie Myths of Australian Military History.* Sydney: University of New South Wales Press Ltd..

Stone G. 2007. *Who Killed Channel 9? The Death of Kerry Packer's Mighty Dream Machine.* Sydney: Pan Macmillan.

Strauss AL, Corbin J. 1990. *Basics of Qualitative Research: Grounded Theory Procedures and Techniques.* Newbury Park: Sage.

Strauss AL, Corbin J. 1998. *Basics of Qualitative Research: Techniques and Procedures for Developing Grounded Theory.* 2nd edn. Newbury Park: Sage.

Submission to the Australian Government's 2010 Review of the Independent Screen Production Sector, 2010. Australian Government Screen Australia.

Surratt, CG. 2001. *Internet and Social Change.* North Carolina: McFarland & Company.

Swift B. 2009. No Conflict, No Interest. *Inside Film.* July: 8 & 38.

Swift B. 2011. *Culture Against Currency in Local Film Survival.* The Drum TV. 11 November.

Swift B. 2012a. SAFC to put FilmLab program on hold to continue screen attraction activities, *Inside Film.* December. http://if.com.au/2012/12/17/article/SAFC-to-put-FilmLab-program-on-hold-to-continue-screen-attraction-activities/XHMKPLXJHX.html.

Swift B. 2012b. Government moves step closer to documentary definition, *Inside Film.* December. http://if.com.au/2012/07/05/article/ZLOITTFLGH.html

Sydow J, Schreyogg G, Koch J. 2005. *Organizational Paths: Path Dependency and Beyond.* 21st EGOS Colloquium, Berlin, 30 June–2 July.

Taylor R, Micolich P, Jonas D. 1999. *Can science be Used to Further Our Understanding of Art?* University of New South Wales. Physics World. October. http://authenticationinart.org/pdf/literature/Fractal-Expressionisme-Can-Science-Be-Used-To-Further-Our-Understanding-Of-Art.docx.pdf

*Tech Trends 2018: The symphonic enterprise.* 2018. Deloitte Insights. https://www2.deloitte.com/insights/us/en/focus/tech-trends/2018.html

Telfer J. 1999. *With greatest expectation: The colony, crime and corrections in South Australia*. Paper presented at the History of Crime, Policing and Punishment Conference convened by the Australian Institute of Criminology in conjunction with Charles Sturt University. Canberra, 9–10 December.

The BBC Reith Lectures. *I found myself in the art world, 2013*. Radio program. ABC Radio National, Sydney, 14 November.

The Kuhn Cycle. 2012. *Thwink.org*. http://www.thwink.org/sustain/glossary/KuhnCycle.htm

The Secret Life of Chaos. 2010. Television program. SBS (Television) on Demand, Sydney. 17 July 2013.

*The Vietnam War. 2017*. Television program. Volume one (episodes 1–5) Volume two (episodes 6–10) PBS Distribution.

The War. 2007. Television program, (episodes 1–7). PBS Distribution.

Thom V. 2007. Australian Film Commission: *Investigation into the Assessment of Film Funding Applications*. Commonwealth Ombudsman. Report no. 2. http://www.ombudsman.gov.au/__data/assets/pdf_file/0025/26296/investigation_2007_02.pdf

Thompson J, Thompson S. 2018. *The Kremlinologist: Llewellyn E Thompson, America's Man in Cold War Moscow*. Baltimore: John Hopkins University Press.

THX. 2013. *The THX story*. THX Ltd. http://www.thx.com/about-us/the-thx-story/

Timmons JA, Spinelli S. 2004. *New Venture Creation: Entrepreneurship in the 21st Century*, 6th edn, New York: McGraw Hill & Irwin.

Toyota. 2020. *Toyota Production System*. Toyota Motor Corporation. https://global.toyota/en/company/vision-and-philosophy/production-system/

Tredennick H, Radice B. 1969. *Plato: The Last Days of Socrates*. Middlesex: Penguin Books.

Turing A. 1937. On Computable Numbers, with an Application to the Entscheidungsproblem, *Proceedings of the London Mathematical Society*. Series 2 42, no. 1: 230–265.

Turing A. 1950. Computing Machinery and Intelligence. *Mind* 59, no. 236: 433–460.

Turing A. 1952. The Chemical Basis of Morphogenesis. *Philosophical Transactions of the Royal Society of London. Series B, Biological Sciences* 237, no. 641: 37–72.

Turow J. 1984. *Media Industries: The Production of News and Entertainment*. New York: Longman.

Vago S. 2009. Irving Fisher: Out of Keynes's Shadow. *The Economist*. 12 February. http://www.economist.com/node/13104022

Van de Ven AH, Polley DE, Garud R, Venkataraman S. 1999. *The Innovation Journey*. New York: Oxford University Press.

Vander Hook S. 2011. *Rupert Murdoch News Corporation Magnate*. Minnesota: ABDO Publishing Company.

Venegas C. 2009. Thinking Regionally: Singular in Diversity and Diverse in Unity. In J Holt & A Perren (eds). *Media Industries: History, Theory, and Method.* Chichester: Wiley-Blackwell: 120–131.

Verhoeven D. 2010. Film, video, DVD and Online Delivery. In S Cunningham & G Turner (eds). *The Media & Communications in Australia.* 3rd edn. Crows Nest: Allen & Unwin: 133–154.

von Bertalanffy L. 1968. *General System Theory: Foundations, Development, Applications.* New York: George Braziller.

von Neumann J, Morgenstern O. 1944. *Theory of Games and Economic Behaviour.* Princeton: Princeton University Press.

Voss V. 1977. *Flying Minnows.* London: Arms & Armour Press.

Ward M. 1995. Butterflies and Bifurcations: Can Chaos Theory Contribute to our Understanding of Family Systems? *Journal of Marriage and Family* 57, no. 3: 629–638.

Ward M. 2001. *Beyond Chaos: The Underlying Theory Behind Life, the Universe and Everything.* New York: St. Martin's Press.

Weber A. 1929. *Theory of the Location of Industries.* Trans C J Friedrich. Chicago: The University of Chicago Press.

Weber A, Hull R. 1948. *Farewell to European History: Or, the Conquest of Nihilism.* New Haven: Yale University Press.

Webster JG, Phalen PF, Lichty LW. 2006. Open letter to students using ratings analysis [Susan D. Whiting, A C Nielsen], and An introduction to audience research. In *Ratings Analysis: The Theory and Practice of Audience Research.* 3rd edn. New Jersey: Lawrence Erlbaum Associates.

Weerakkody N. 2008. *Research Methods for Media and Communication.* Melbourne: Oxford University Press.

Weightman G. 2001. *The Frozen Water Trade.* London: Harper Collins Publishers.

Weir D. 2013. *How Sustainable is the Australian Content Production Industry?* Keynote address presented at the Australian International Documentary Conference. Adelaide, 25–28 February.

Welch J. 2001. *What I've Learned Leading a Great Company and Great People.* London: Headline Book Publishing.

Wells HG. 1971. *The Outline of History.* New York: Doubleday and Company.

Wilkins G. 2013. Innovation will Shape our Future, says Rupert Murdoch. *The Sydney Morning Herald.* Business Day. 1 November. http://www.smh.com.au/business/the-economy/innovation-will-shape-our-future-says-rupert-murdoch-20131101-2wmib.html

Willis B. 2013. Film Funding Will Have a Sharper Focus in Future. *The Advertiser.* 24 September, p. 37.

Winters RD. 2006. *Beyond Band of Brothers.* New York: Penguin Group.

Wittenberg J. 2010. *What is a Historical Legacy?* Washington: American Political Science Association.

Wohlleben P. 2016. *The Hidden Life of Trees: What They feel, How they Communicate – Discoveries From a Secret World.*

Wohlleben P. 2016. *The Hidden Life of Trees: What They feel, How they Communicate – Discoveries From a Secret World.* Carlton: Black Inc.

Wollstonecraft Shelley M. 2014. *Frankenstein.* New York: Millennium Publications.

Wood D. 2009. Real Life Access to Second Life Worlds: The Potential, the Problems and the Possibilities for a Barrier-Free Future. *The International Journal of Diversity in Organisations, Communities and Nations* 8, no. 6:139–148.

Wood D. 2010. Communicating in Virtual Worlds Through a Web 2.0 Application. *Telecommunications Journal of Australia.* Monash University Press 60, no. 2: 19.1–19.16.

Woodman H. 1972. Economic History and Economic Theory: The New Economic History in America. *Journal of Interdisciplinary History* 3, no. 2: 323–350.

Woods J. 1997. Royal Commission into the New South Wales Police Service: Final Report Volume 1: *Corruption.* The Government of the State of New South Wales, Sydney.

Woolf V. 1977. *A Room of One's Own.* 9th reprint. London: The Hogarth Press Ltd.

WWF Global. 2013. *Impact of Habitat Loss of Species.* World Wildlife Fund Global. https://wwf.panda.org/discover/our_focus/wildlife_practice/problems/habitat_loss_degradation/

Zolin R, Kropp F. 2008. Public or Private by Genetics of Design?: A Case Study of Organizational Design Decisions for New Public Ventures, *The International Public Management Review (IPMR)* 9, no. 1: 130–147.

Zolin R, Kropp F. 2009. *How Environmental and Organizational Complexity Affects Opportunity Recognition in Development Projects.* CINet. http://eprints.qut.edu.au/27165/1/CINet_09_-_Zolin.pdf

Zolin R, Kropp F. 2010. How Environmental and Organizational Complexity Affects Opportunity Recognition and Exploitation in Development Projects. *Proceedings of the 7th AGSE International Entrepreneurship Research Exchange.* 2–5 February. University of the Sunshine Coast. Queensland.

# Index


**A**

Abnormal, 110
Action research, 66–68, 74, 78
Actor, 23, 43, 44, 63, 70, 77, 89, 91, 93, 101
Adelaide Entrepreneurial Ecosystem (AEE), 19, 117
Aldrin, Buzz, 35
*Alita: Battle Angel*, 112
Ares Vallis, 57
Armstrong, Neil (1930-2012), 35
Artificial intelligence/intelligent (AI), 29, 30, 40, 92
Astronaut, 35
Augment/augmented/augmentation, 28–30, 40, 41, 56, 57, 66, 101, 103
Augmented reality (AR), 56
Australian Broadcasting Corporation (ABC), 26, 61, 62, 77, 106
Avant-garde, 87

**B**

Bacon, Francis (1561-1626), 21, 57, 123
Balsamic moon, 30, 31
Barnes Dance/Barnes Dance Principle, 68–71
Barnes, Henry (1906-1968), 68
Barney, Jay, 46
Bioplastics, 91
*Bladerunner/Bladerunner 2049*, 112
Bligh, William (1754-1817), 14–16
Blundstone, 19
Bounty, His Majesty's Ship, 14, 16
Byron, Lord George Gordon (1788-1824), 29

**C**

Cash Flow, 78
Celestial, 35, 38
Churchill, Winston (1874-1965), 54, 55, 57, 121



G. A. Reed, *Entrepreneurs Navigating a Universe of Disruption*, https://doi.org/10.1007/978-981-19-0703-6

Cold War, 12, 34, 35, 54, 112
Collins, Michael (1930-2021), 35
Computer mediated reality (CMR), 56, 66, 78, 88, 101, 111
Conflict, 11, 25, 38, 41, 44, 73, 89, 90
Cook, James (1728-1779), 15
Cosmological constant, 32, 46
Cosmonaut, 35
Csikszentmihalyi, Mihaly, 21–23
Cuban Missile Crisis, 12
Cultural nationalism, 111
Cultural normative behaviours, 111
Curiosity rover, 57, 59
Cusp, 46, 87, 101

**D**

*The Day the Earth Stood Still*, 112
Dent, Norman (1963-1991), 27
Deoxyribonucleic acid (DNA), 30, 72
Department of State Development, 6, 31
Design thinking, 4, 11, 103, 107
Diagonal crossing, 42, 55
Diesel Kiki, 6, 7, 9
Disruption, 36, 47, 88–90, 106–108, 113, 116, 123

**E**

Earth, 12, 35, 37, 38, 40, 41, 57, 60, 89, 110, 121, 122
Earth-based, 40, 41, 57
Eilat, 19
Einstein, Albert (1879-1955), 32, 44, 46, 68
*Entrepreneur*, 1–4, 8, 13, 14, 16, 18, 21, 31–34, 36–39, 46, 47, 56, 57, 61, 66, 70–72, 91, 101–104, 116, 117, 119, 122
Entrepreneurial, 1–4, 14, 15, 20, 26, 31–35, 38, 43, 55–57, 61, 66, 78, 88–90, 102–104, 108, 111, 115–117, 119, 121, 123
Environment, 4, 19, 20, 32, 33, 39, 43, 47, 55–57, 60, 61, 87–92, 102–104, 106–109, 113, 115–117, 119, 122
Ethical, 12, 40, 89, 108, 110, 112, 123
*Ex_Machina* (2014), 112
*Extremis*, 15

**F**

*Flow*, 23
Flow of Time, 122
Fourth Industrial Revolution, 1, 29, 30, 36, 40, 56, 57, 87, 89, 107, 123
Foxtel, 26, 77
Fractals, 92, 95–97
*Frankenstein*, 28–30
Frederickson, Barbara, 21

**G**

Global, 3, 5, 18, 29, 31, 34, 36, 42, 56, 60, 78, 87–89, 95, 102, 123, 124
The Great Depression, 41
Greece, 19
Gut instinct, 30

**H**

Hercules Powder Company, 38
Hippocrates (460-370 BCE), 30, 38
Human-centred design, 5, 8, 11, 89
Human society, 13, 41, 56, 90, 106
Human species, 32, 109

I
Inflationary, 40, 47, 55
Intangibility, 4, 30, 32, 38, 46, 47
Intangible/s, 2, 27, 32, 38, 39, 44, 47, 53, 110, 113
Intersection, 33, 34, 42, 43, 68, 72
Intrapreneur, 34, 36, 102
Intrapreneurial, 5, 26, 34, 35, 78
Israel, 24
Interactions, 42, 68, 103, 104, 123

J
Jobs, Steve (1955-2011), 17

K
Kennedy, John Fitzgerald (JFK) (1917-1963), 12, 34, 41
Khrushchev, Nikita (1894-1971), 12
King Gee, 19
Kuhn, Thomas (1922-1996), 27, 28, 36, 37

L
Lean manufacturing, 8, 57, 88, 109
Lean methodology, 89, 109
Lincoln, Abraham (1809-1865), 54
Lovelace, Ada (1815-1852), 29
Lunar surface, 35

M
Macarthur, John (1767-1834), 14, 16, 18
Machine learning (ML), 40, 41, 111
Mandelbrot, Benoit (Professor) (1924-2010), 3, 92, 97
Mandelbrot set, 3, 95, 96
Manifesto, 3, 13, 66
Marketing, 3
Mars, 57
Mars Hand Lens Imager (MAHLI), 59
Mars rover, 59
Mars shot, 89
Matter, 3, 8, 29, 32, 46, 75, 91
Metaphor, 43, 47, 68, 95
Metaphorical, 37, 94–96
*Metropolis* (1927), 112
Milky Way Galaxy, 22, 38, 39
*Missing: Presumed Dead*, 25, 26, 30, 72, 75, 77, 78
Mixed reality (MR), 56, 101
*The Modern Prometheus*, 28, 29
Moon, 29–31, 89
Moon shot, 34, 89
Moral injury, 12

N
National Aeronautics and Space Administration (NASA), 35, 37, 41, 57, 59
Navigate, 32, 36, 47, 72
New abnormal, 110
*New lean*, 89
New worlds, 60
NeXT Computer, Inc./NeXT Inc., 17, 18
*Nine Women of Northfield: Tales from within*, 77
Nuclear, 34, 35

O
Off-Earth, 29, 34, 36, 40, 60, 89
Open boat, 14, 15

**P**

*Parabolic scramble*, 4, 8, 10, 13, 30, 42, 44, 46, 47, 55, 56, 66, 68–72, 74, 76, 77, 88–96, 101–108, 111–113, 115–119, 123
Paradigm, 31, 37
Path dependency, 43, 64, 74, 75, 77, 104, 117
Path dependent, 63, 72, 90, 91, 117
Pathfinder, 58, 77
Pathfinder rover, 57
Pedestrian/s, 34, 42, 43, 55, 68–70, 93
Penrose, Edith (1914-1996), 38
Penrosian, 40, 44, 46
*Persistent destruction*, 18
Peterson, Christopher, 21
Planetary, 35, 36, 38, 57, 87, 90
Pollack, Jackson (1912-1956), 2, 3, 60, 95, 96
Polymers, 91
Positive psychology, 21
Power dynamics, 110
Prototypes, 5, 6

**Q**

Quantum computing, 29, 88, 89, 111

**R**

Redefine/redefined/redefinition, 74, 89, 90, 93, 116
Reductive, 33, 41, 110, 117
Relativity, 44
Risk/s, 2, 4, 14, 18, 27, 28, 31–35, 56, 102–105, 109
Roosevelt, Franklin Delano (FDR) (1882-1945), 41

**S**

Samos, Island of, 19, 20
Schwarzchild, Karl (1873-1916), 44
Scientific method, 21, 35, 57, 60, 128
Scramble crossing, 42–45, 55, 68–70, 72, 93, 95
Scrambling, 72, 106
Screen Australia, 26, 61, 65, 77
Semi-conductor, 29, 87
Shackleton, Ernest (1874-1922), 15, 16
Shelley, Percy (1792-1822), 29
SIDK, 6
Smiths Industries Pty Ltd, 121
Sojourner, 57, 58
Solar cycle, 91, 122
Solar system, 35, 37, 39, 57
Souveniring, 11
Space, 32–40, 47, 57, 60, 72, 89, 91, 121, 122
Space Shuttle, 121
Spectra, 2, 110
Start-up, 4, 30, 31, 60, 91, 107, 111, 117
Straight-talk, 75–77, 120, 121
Swiss Patent Office, 44

**T**

Taba, 19
Tahiti, 14
Thompson, Llewellyn 'Tommy' (1904-1972), 12
Timor, 14
Toyota Production System, 8, 88, 109

**U**

Union of Soviet Socialist Republics (USSR), 12
United States of America (USA), 12, 34, 54, 68

Universe, 4, 32, 34–37, 40, 41, 46, 47, 53, 55, 57, 60, 68, 87, 116

V
Vehicular, 34, 36, 43, 55
Vietnam War (1955-1975), 12
Virtual reality (VR), 56
Voyager probes, 37, 38, 40, 41, 53

W
Washington, 27, 59
Wollstonecraft Shelley, Mary (1797-1851), 28–30

FSC
www.fsc.org
MIX
Papier | Fördert gute Waldnutzung
FSC® C083411

Kolibri 360 GmbH
Ferdinand-Jühlke-Straße 7
99095 Erfurt, Deutschland
produktsicherheit@kolibri360.de